T0330541

Promise, Pitfalls, and Potential of Social Entrepreneurship

This book dives into the heart of social entrepreneurship as the authors share the latest research, global experiences, authentic private conversations, and diverse narratives around this widely popular concept.

The idea and practice of social entrepreneurship has swept the world, taken up with enthusiasm by business leaders, nonprofit practitioners, and public policy makers alike. In this book, the authors argue that social entrepreneurship is surrounded by great promise, and that this high expectation has contributed to its pitfalls, setting it out as separate and different from other kinds of nonprofit organising, public service provision, and business for social benefit. After exploring the problem of inflated expectations, the authors rescue the concept from perfection – overly positive normative judgements – by presenting practical ways forward.

The book sets out how to really unleash the power of social entrepreneurship so that it can actually deliver on its promise to improve how we organise for social purpose. This potential revolves around four key themes that are levers for social change: innovative individuals, social impact, scaling social enterprises, and the power of ecosystems. Through these themes, the book covers a wide range of approaches to social enterprise illustrated by specific examples and experiences from five continents.

This accessible book is a valuable resource for a variety of practitioners, upper-level students, instructors, and business scholars, particularly those with an interest in social/environmental impact, entrepreneurship, business ethics, sustainable business, ESG and CSR.

Sheila Cannon is Assistant Professor in Social Entrepreneurship at Trinity Business School, Trinity College Dublin, Ireland. She is Director of Engagement at the Trinity Centre for Social Innovation. She publishes research on and teaches about the third sector including social enterprises, nonprofits, and civil society organisations. Her research contributes to knowledge on how organisations influence and respond to sociocultural change. She worked in peacebuilding for 12 years in southeast Europe and Northern Ireland and is chair of the board of the social enterprise, Shuttle Knit. She has a bachelor's degree in Ancient Greek from Vassar College, New York.

Concepción Galdón is IE Business School's Vice-Dean for Business with Purpose and Director of IE Foundation's Center for Social Innovation and Sustainability. Concepción teaches sustainable business, social entrepreneurship, and sustainable innovation and technology. Concepción is also president of the social venture Puentes Global, which she co-founded in 2009 and has collaborated in several civil society initiatives aimed at fostering business with purpose. Concepción is an economist at Universidad Autónoma de Madrid. She holds a Master in Public Administration and International Development from Harvard Kennedy School and a PhD in International Economy and Development from Universidad Complutense de Madrid.

Routledge CoBS Focus on Responsible Business
Series Editors: Tom Gamble and Adrián Zicari
The Council on Business and Society (CoBS)

This series is published in collaboration with the Council on Business & Society (CoBS).

Routledge CoBS Focus on Responsible Business provides international and multicultural perspectives on responsible leadership and business practices in line with the UN SDGs. Contributors from leading business schools on 4 continents offer local, cultural and global perspectives on the issues covered, drawing on high level research and transformed into engaging and digestible content for students, academics and practitioners.

Topics include but are not limited to: responsible finance and accounting, CSR and governance, supply chain management, leadership, diversity and inclusion, performance and innovation, responsible management, and wellbeing at work.

For more information about this series, please visit: www.routledge.com

Promise, Pitfalls, and Potential of Social Entrepreneurship

Positive Change Unleashed

Sheila Cannon and Concepción Galdón

Routledge
Taylor & Francis Group

LONDON AND NEW YORK

First published 2024
by Routledge
4 Park Square, Milton Park, Abingdon, Oxon OX14 4RN

and by Routledge
605 Third Avenue, New York, NY 10158

Routledge is an imprint of the Taylor & Francis Group, an informa business

© 2024 Sheila Cannon and Concepción Galdón

The right of Sheila Cannon and Concepción Galdón to be identified as authors of this work has been asserted in accordance with sections 77 and 78 of the Copyright, Designs and Patents Act 1988.

British Library Cataloguing-in-Publication Data
A catalogue record for this book is available from the British Library

ISBN: 978-1-032-51997-5 (hbk)
ISBN: 978-1-032-53009-3 (pbk)
ISBN: 978-1-003-40969-4 (ebk)

DOI: 10.4324/9781003409694

Typeset in Times New Roman
by Apex CoVantage, LLC

Contents

Introduction

A Journey of Theory, Practice, and Impact

One year ago today, we decided to embark on a journey to explore the promise, the pitfalls, and pathways into the future of social entrepreneurship. We had never met in person, although we co-authored an article for the Council on Business & Society (CoBS). We were overworked, overwhelmed, . . . we could go on with words that start with "over." So, when we got the proposal from the CoBS to write this book, we were well-equipped with reasons not to do it. But we had one good reason to go for it. We felt an urgent need to write publicly about those things that we have been discussing over coffee or beers with so many social entrepreneurs and other practitioners for so many years that often are not part of the public discourses. We wanted to explore a more complete narrative about the wondrous (and arduous) journey of organising for social change. And, as Lady Gaga put it in *Million Reasons*, you often only need one good reason to stay.

Over the past three decades, the concept of social enterprise has swept the world, taken up with enthusiasm by business leaders, nonprofit practitioners, and public policymakers alike. We know that social enterprise holds tremendous promise. However, these lofty expectations have contributed to its pitfalls, isolating it as something distinct from traditional businesses, separate from public service initiatives, and with different organisational structures. In this book, we're not here to burst anyone's bubble. We are certain that social entrepreneurship can be a powerful part of societal change across all three sectors, but we need to be open about its present hurdles to make it so.

You see, we didn't set out to write a textbook or academic research piece on how to set up a social enterprise. No, we wanted to invite you into our world to share our experiences, questions, way of thinking about these matters, and most importantly, our doubts and hopes for the future. So here is a disclaimer for our university colleagues: Don't expect complete literature reviews and rigorously crafted theory development depicted in careful language. Here's just us, standing on the shoulders of giants when helpful, but ultimately us. Feel free to agree or disagree. To like it or not.

As you might have guessed, this book is not mostly for academics but for changemakers of all kinds, from loud innovators to quiet service delivery

DOI: 10.4324/9781003409694-1

agents. Whether you're an advanced student, a consultant, coach, educator, or practitioner in the fields of social entrepreneurship, sustainable business, or community development, we wrote this book to spark your thinking. We invite you to explore the multifaceted world of social entrepreneurship, uncover its potential, and join us in the quest to positively impact society.

Methodology: Drawing from Literature, Experience, and Inspiring Conversations

Our approach to this book is rooted in our collective experiences and marked by a deep appreciation for the voices of the social entrepreneurs and other practitioners in the social entrepreneurship ecosystems who have inspired us. We are, first and foremost, enthusiasts in the field of social entrepreneurship. The stories, insights, and thoughts we share here are drawn from the countless hours we've spent in the trenches, working alongside social entrepreneurs, and experiencing their journeys firsthand through the social enterprises in which we are also personally involved. While this is not an academic book in the traditional sense, literature has an important role to play so that our arguments are supported by a larger evidence base. However, our goal is not to inundate you with academic jargon or exhaustive citations. Instead, we aim to bring the literature to life, making it accessible and relevant to all readers. But also, as academics ourselves, we take a critical view. We are not blind advocates of social entrepreneurship. On the contrary, and like many of the social entrepreneurs we have worked with, we see many of the problems, weaknesses, and challenges. Otherwise, this would be a very short book.

In our quest to offer a richer, more human understanding of social entrepreneurship, we've conducted interviews with a variety of social entrepreneurs and those who support social enterprises. Their voices, heard throughout the book, offer insights into their day to day. We're profoundly thankful to each one of them for sharing their stories and experiences. They did their best to help us; any shortcomings of this book are ours, not theirs. We would like to encourage you to check out their work. You'll be fascinated. They are:

- Rodrigo Baggio, Founder and CEO of Recode: Recode encourages a new consciousness in individuals and organisations to ethically appropriate new technologies to create solutions that positively impact society. They facilitate education spaces that empower people and help them develop skills and solve social problems in Brazil and 11 other countries (www. recode.org.br).
- Maria Baryamujura, Founder and CEO of Community Base Tourism Initiative (COBATI): COBATI enables individuals to leverage their culture and livelihoods for tourism-related benefits. Through this nonprofit, Maria

fosters sustainable rural lifestyles while diversifying tourism offerings to tap into Uganda's growing tourism sector (www.cobatiuganda.org).

- Catalina Escobar, Founder and CEO of Fundación Juanfe: Based in Colombia, Fundación Juanfe invests in physical, mental, and emotional health; in education; and in the employability of young mothers in situations of extreme poverty and vulnerability in Cartagena and Medellín (www.juanfe.org).
- Chris MM Gordon, CEO and co-founder of Irish Social Enterprise Network (ISEN), the umbrella support organisation for social enterprises in Ireland, and Managing Partner of Collaboration Ireland. He chairs the board of Far and Wild, a sustainable eco-tourism adventure company. Chris was the first Country Partner for BCorp Ireland and manages several pan-European social enterprise initiatives (www.chrismmgordon.com).
- João Magalhães, Founder and CEO of Code For All and Ubbu: Code For All empowers adults through technological education, irrespective of their past educational level or background (www.codeforall.com). Ubbu is a learning tool that teaches computer science and programming to kids (www.ubbu.io). Both companies are based in Portugal.
- Nguyen Thi Le Na, Founder and CEO of Cam Vinh Ky Yen organic orange farm in Nghe An, Viet Nam. Le Na trains and supports local farmers in sustainable ecological practices to avoid soil depletion and reduce waste. She distributes oranges as well as orange-based products including tea, essential oils, and sweets, via Phu Quy Agricultural Farm Joint Stock Company which she established to increase sales of all the farms in her community, contributing to the development of her region (https://dacsancamvinh.net/).
- Dr David Nyaluke, Head of Education at Proudly Made in Africa (PMIA), with the aim of raising awareness among future business leaders of the historic problems and opportunities of doing business in Africa. PMIA has two objectives: To bring African perspectives and voices into Irish universities, and to support African businesses to bring their products into European markets (www.proudlymadeinafrica.org).
- Javier Pita, Founder and CEO of NaviLens: NaviLens is a company that helps the visually impaired, who have difficulty using traditional signage, be autonomous in unfamiliar environments. Based in Spain, NaviLens has expanded internationally to the United Kingdom (UK) and the United States (USA) (www.navilens.com).
- Killian Stokes, Co-founder of Moyee Coffee, that takes an innovative approach to fixing the coffee value chain to make it more fair for farmers. Moyee developed and models FairChain, where the value and profit of the coffee can be traced clearly by the consumer through block chain technology. Moyee set up coffee manufacturing near the coffee farms so that communities gain more value from their product. Killian is also the CEO of Proudly Made in Africa (www.moyeecoffee.com; www.moyeeethiopia.com).

- Elizabeth Suda, Founder and CEO of Article 22, a jewellery company that recovers munitions (remains of landmines) from Laos, employs artisans in Laos to make jewellery, and sells the products globally, based out of New York City and Paris. She employs the artisans, raises awareness of landmines, and uses the profits to help clear remaining landmines in Laos (www.article22.com).

It is important to note that this book is a reflection of how we see things, shaped by our experiences, conversations we've had over the years, and the literature we've reviewed. Certainly, our perspective is not the only one, not always the best one. We acknowledge our biases. To begin with, we are both European and we both work at business schools. As much as we have tried hard to take a broad view, we are certain to come with limitations, which you as a reader will probably pick out much more clearly than we do.

We don't expect to close any debate, but rather to open many. Our hope is that this book serves as a catalyst for interesting conversations, and even disagreements. We encourage you to question our views, challenge our assumptions, and contribute to the ever-evolving narrative of social entrepreneurship. As we dive into the following pages, we invite you to be an active participant in this journey, drawing from your own experiences and perspectives.

Environmental and Social Goals

One pivotal test that social entrepreneurship faces is how it relates to the most pervasive existential challenge of our time – the environmental crisis, the term we use here to refer to the myriad ways that humans are damaging nature, including but not limited to global warming, ocean acidification, and biodiversity loss (Ripple et al., 2020). Ironically, the threats we pose to nature are a problem for which we are not short of solutions. For example, if you go to the Drawdown.org website or pick up the book with the same name, you can find the top 100 solutions using existing technology to reduce carbon dioxide emissions ranked in order of cost-effectiveness, put together by a coalition of scientists, policymakers, and other experts (Hawken, 2017). Similarly, a wealth of scientific research is going into materials and processes to foster circularity to avoid waste and ways to protect biodiversity. In other words, from a biophysical point of view, we are accelerating our knowledge on reducing environmental damage due to human activity and developing the necessary tools (arguably, not quickly enough).

What is missing from this and many other "solutions" to the environmental crisis is how to bring about the social changes required to make these solutions feasible for all. The impact of the environmental crisis and responses to it are unevenly divided, exacerbating inequality. The concept of Climate Justice (Schlosberg, 2012) shows the inseparable relationship between social and environmental goals. Those who bear the least responsibility for the environmental crisis are the ones who will be most negatively affected by it, and by the responses, such as changing industries and the resulting job losses. It is paramount to foster a sustainable, socially just transition. And who knows something about organising for social change? That's right. Social entrepreneurs.

So why has there been a disconnect between social entrepreneurship and environmental action to date? Well, we think there is not one simple reason, but several influencing factors. An underlying dynamic is that environmental and social goals and initiatives have been treated as separate areas, with separate issues, and separate solutions in a general sense as a result of humans seeing themselves as separate from nature (Leichenko & O'Brien, 2019). More specifically, the study and practice of environmental entrepreneurship evolved in parallel and disconnected from social entrepreneurship (Vedula et al., 2022). Furthermore, in both nonprofit and for-profit studies overall, there is evidence that the environmental crisis has been treated as separate to social issues and concerns.

In nonprofit studies, environmental missions are one type of social mission. In the largest international comparative study of nonprofits, mission themes are divided into areas such as education, health, social services, advocacy, environment, etc. (Salamon & Anheier, 1997). Environmental missions tend to include advocacy, conservation, and development work (Kagan & Dodge, 2022). This categorisation of environmental goals as a type of social goal to some extent makes sense: Is there a stronger social goal than preserving the planet in which all people live? However, the environmental crisis shows that the natural environment concerns every social goal. Rather than one type of goal, the environmental crisis is the context in which all other goals need to be considered and addressed.

In for-profit studies, corporate social responsibility includes social performance that has evolved separately and disconnected from corporate environmentalism, or the greening of the firm (Linnenluecke & Griffiths, 2013). This greening only emerged later in the 1990s in response to the environmental movement that created pressure for the companies to respond (ibid). Furthermore, corporate sustainability has tended to interpret the climate crisis as an organisational challenge, misconstruing the severity and scope of the issue into something much more manageable (Wright & Nyberg, 2017). For practitioners of corporate sustainability this organisational approach may have been a practical way to address the enormity of the environmental crisis. But as a result, businesses are often criticised for not taking the crisis seriously enough and prioritising profit over planet.

We suspect that in research the distinction between social and environmental has been stricter than in practice. Following the lead of many social entrepreneurs, we propose taking an integrated approach, one that more consciously considers the relationship between social and environmental aspects. Firstly, there are many social entrepreneurs who are dedicating their energy and careers to addressing the climate crisis (Vickers & Lyon, 2012). Notably, Nature-Based Enterprises are essentially social enterprises with an environmental mission (Kooijman et al., 2021). And certainly, the Sustainable Development Goals bring together in one comprehensive framework social and environmental goals that all actors and organisations can align their goals and initiatives with. Policymakers are also keeping track of how the 17 goals interact with each other (Nilsson et al., 2016), thus considering the interdependent relationship between social and environmental factors.

Box 0.1 Maria Baryamujura, COBATI

Community tourism is very important for women. When they sell their crafts, their work feeds into the community. They can provide lunch and textbooks for their children or go to a Health Centre to deliver their babies safely. This costs little money, which they usually don't have, but through Homestead tourism, they started generating income to afford payment for such basic needs. We trained them to protect their environment. They take their children to the wetlands in the village. They say: "We look after the wetland because that's where we get the clay to make our pots," because that community is known for their pottery which brings in income. Now you see the relationship. Now we are into conservation. Now we are into climate change advocacy.

The environmental crisis shows how important social entrepreneurship is. It is a critical part of responding to climate change because it combines bottom-up community organising, with the power of business, with skills and tools of social change. Environmental scientists have gathered the data, analysed the trends, and communicated what we need to change. Engineers have already developed a plethora of solutions. Intergovernmental bodies have set out what we need to do. Advocates have disrupted events and raised awareness of the issue. Businesses have the resources and power to make significant change and will play an important role. We need all hands on deck. The environmental crisis won't wait, and neither should we. Social entrepreneurship can and should be a critical part of the solution, but we must engage in challenging conversations now to harness its full power.

In conclusion, when we talk about social entrepreneurship and social missions, within those terms we include environmental missions, because you cannot separate out concerns of the natural environment from social issues. As we seem to forget, humans are part of nature. Furthermore, when we talk about any social enterprise, there is always a consideration that the work involved impacts on the natural environment in some way, whether that is overt and deliberate or unstated. As you will see, this integrated approach is taken by our social entrepreneurs and social enterprises included in this book.

A Glimpse into What Lies Ahead

We've structured our book into three distinct parts:

1. The Promise: In this part, we'll explore the various approaches to social enterprise, how and why we all became so excited about it. What do we know about social entrepreneurs, social enterprises, their support ecosystems, and their capacity to bring about impact at scale? Here is where we lay the foundation of what social enterprise can be and the hope it represents.
2. The Pitfalls: Here, we delve into the challenges and the unrealistic expectations surrounding social enterprise. In this part, we'll scrutinise the normative judgements that sometimes lead social enterprise astray. It's our critical examination, where we identify the hurdles that have sometimes hindered its progress.
3. The Potential: This is where we pivot towards proposed solutions. We present options to overcome the limitations and realise the full potential of social enterprise. We aim to "rescue" the concept of social enterprise from "perfection" by presenting ways forward that work with the reality and diversity of social enterprises.

We started this introduction by discussing how and why we decided to write the book you have in front of you right now. A year after that commitment, we sit together in a coffee shop with the freedom to put everything we discuss on these pages, the comfortable and the uncomfortable. So, grab a seat and join us as we embark on this journey through the highs and lows, through the collision of idealism and reality, and the relentless pursuit of a better world in the face of some really wicked problems. Welcome to our world, the world of social entrepreneurship.

References

Hawken, P. (Ed.). (2017). *Drawdown: The most comprehensive plan ever proposed to reverse global warming*. Penguin Books.

Kagan, J. A., & Dodge, J. (2022). The third sector and climate change: A literature review and agenda for future research and action. *Nonprofit and Voluntary Sector Quarterly, 52*(4). https://doi.org/10.1177/08997640221123587

Kooijman, E. D., McQuaid, S., Rhodes, M.-L., Collier, M. J., & Pilla, F. (2021). Innovating with nature: From nature-based solutions to nature-based enterprises. *Sustainability, 13*(3). https://doi.org/10.3390/su13031263

Leichenko, R. M., & O'Brien, K. L. (2019). *Climate and society: Transforming the future*. Polity.

Linnenluecke, M. K., & Griffiths, A. (2013). Firms and sustainability: Mapping the intellectual origins and structure of the corporate sustainability field. *Global Environmental Change, 23*(1), 382–391. https://doi.org/10.1016/j.gloenvcha.2012.07.007

Nilsson, M., Griggs, D., & Visbeck, M. (2016). Policy: Map the interactions between sustainable development goals. *Nature, 534*(7607), 320–322. https://doi.org/10.1038/534320a

Ripple, W. J., Wolf, C., Newsome, T. M., Barnard, P., & Moomaw, W. R. (2020). World scientists' warning of a climate emergency. *BioScience, 70*(1), 8–12. Academic Search Complete.

Salamon, L. M., & Anheier, H. K. (1997). *Defining the nonprofit sector: A cross national analysis*. Manchester University Press.

Schlosberg, D. (2012). Climate justice and capabilities: A framework for adaptation policy. *Ethics & International Affairs, 26*(4), 445–461. Cambridge Core. https://doi.org/10.1017/S0892679412000615

Vedula, S., Doblinger, C., Pacheco, D., York, J. G., Bacq, S., Russo, M. V., & Dean, T. J. (2022). Entrepreneurship for the public good: A review, critique, and path forward for social and environmental entrepreneurship research. *Academy of Management Annals, 16*(1), 391–425. https://doi.org/10.5465/annals.2019.0143

Vickers, I., & Lyon, F. (2012). Beyond green niches? Growth strategies of environmentally-motivated social enterprises. *International Small Business Journal, 32*(4), 449–470. https://doi.org/10.1177/0266242612457700

Wright, C., & Nyberg, D. (2017). An inconvenient truth: How organizations translate climate change into business as usual. *Academy of Management Journal, 60*(5), 1633–1661. https://doi.org/10.5465/amj.2015.0718

Part 1

The Promise

1 The Historical Emergence of Social Enterprise

Social entrepreneurship is undoubtedly a powerful way to generate solutions to social and environmental challenges at scale (Bacq & Janssen, 2011; Martin & Osberg, 2007; Weerawardena & Mort, 2006; Nicholls, 2006; Defourny & Nyssens, 2010; Santos, 2012; Welsh, 2012). Precisely this potential is what makes social entrepreneurship the relevant topic it is today and, likely, the reason you care enough about it to be reading this book. The term "social entrepreneurship" started to be used in the 1980s, but social entrepreneurship has existed in one form or another since well before the expression was coined to refer to it (Dearlove, 2004; Roberts & Woods, 2005).

Florence Nightingale is one of the first paradigmatic examples of a social entrepreneur (Hoogendoorn et al., 2010). This Victorian nurse reduced the mortality rate at the hospital she led in Istanbul from 43% to 2% by applying the management skills she had learned in previous jobs (Bornstein, 2007). In Boston, at the end of the nineteenth century, Reverend Edgar J. Helms founded a charity market where he sold second-hand items that had been repaired by the migrants in poverty whom he aimed to support. In 1956, Father José María Arizmendi founded Mondragón Corporación Cooperativa (MCC) in Spain to reduce unemployment in the town, Mondragón, where he served as a priest.

Their stories resonate nicely with the first mention of this topic in the literature in Young's book *If Not for Profit, for What?* published in 1983, in which he talks about "nonprofit entrepreneurship" (Young, 1983). These, and many more worldwide, are examples of mission-driven people who apply innovative solutions, often leveraging private sector management skills, to solve the problems they deeply care about.

Nowadays, the words "social entrepreneurship" are broadly used – arguably, not by everyone on the street. It might not be the kind of thing you discuss with your neighbours in the elevator. Still, it is broadly used by those proactively working to solve social and environmental problems in many countries. You can imagine what a diverse crowd that is. The challenge is that when they use the words "social entrepreneurship," different people assign different meanings to them (Hoogendoorn et al., 2010). Put otherwise, the mental image that comes to their mind when they use the term is not the same.

DOI: 10.4324/9781003409694-3

This is a problem for researchers (in academia, definitions matter a lot), but it is no small challenge for practitioners either. Solving prevalent social and environmental challenges requires all actors to work together. But working together when we mean different things by using the same words is difficult. It's the grown-up version of playing Broken Telephone!

For starters, since "entrepreneurship" is in the term, it would be logical to consider that social entrepreneurship must be a form of "entrepreneurship" (Austin et al., 2006; Dees, 1998a, 1998b). Following the previous logic, those whose mental image of an entrepreneur is the founder of a Silicon Valley high-growth startup might assume that social entrepreneurship must then be the same thing, but with a social/environmental mission. Well, it's more complicated than that. Taking the opposite logic, since "social" is in the term, would all founders of social/environmental mission-oriented organisations be social entrepreneurs? Again, it's complicated.

The origin of this mess is partly the fact that social entrepreneurship as a concept, once it started to pick up towards the end of the twentieth century, took root in different traditions in different parts of the world and different topic areas. Depending on the tradition in which you have evolved academically and professionally, you will attach different characteristics to it that are "obvious" and even "natural" to you. But what is obvious and natural for others who have grown up in a different tradition will be different. Interestingly, neither you nor the others might be aware of the existence of these various traditions or know the one to which you owe your mental structure, the glasses through which you look at social entrepreneurship.

The different historical traditions in which social entrepreneurship evolved in each of the two geographic regions that have mostly led the debate, the United States (USA) and Europe, partly explain the difficulty in agreeing on one definition (Hoogendoorn et al., 2010; Defourny & Nyssens, 2012; Bacq & Janssen, 2011; Defourny & Nyssens, 2010; Galera & Borzaga, 2009; Nicholls, 2006; Weerawardena & Mort, 2006).

The European Tradition: Job Creation and Working with Government

In Europe, during the 1970s and 1980s, high unemployment combined with reduced public budgets put government-led social policies at a stretch. Nonprofits wanted to help. But to foster the labour inclusion of vulnerable people, they needed to reconsider their role and develop new strategies (Hoogendoorn et al., 2010). These new strategies involved implementing activities with a clear social mission but were often carried out through private sector approaches focused on employment generation. However, these employment initiatives did not necessarily involve financing the operation exclusively through market mechanisms. Depending on the specific context of the different countries, different approaches emerged (Defourny & Nyssens, 2010):

Second labour market: Countries like Belgium, France, Germany, and Ireland were home to large, government-funded nonprofits that traditionally acted as intermediaries to provide social services. The second labour market consisted of social service-related organisations creating jobs with the double-fold goal of alleviating unemployment and helping reduce the need for public spending on social policy. In these countries, the law allowed associations and other legal forms of nonprofits to buy and sell products and services in the market (Galera & Borzaga, 2009). Eventually, creating community-led companies with a social mission, mainly for labour inclusion of vulnerable people, became rather popular. For example, in 1983, Ireland created the Community Enterprise Programme, offering funding, training, and support to these companies (O'Hara, 2001).

The cooperative movement and social cooperatives: In countries where the government (in the case of the Nordic countries) or other institutions such as families or the church (in the case of southern countries) had traditionally centralised social assistance, nonprofits didn't have a big infrastructure and the law greatly limited the commercial activities of associations (Galera & Borzaga, 2009). In this context, second labour market solutions were not possible. In some of these European countries, cooperatives had a long-standing tradition. Without big nonprofits, cooperatives began to be created to integrate excluded groups into the labour market in various sectors. These cooperatives are called "social cooperatives" (Defourny & Nyssens, 2017).

Quasi-market solutions: In this system, developed in the United Kingdom (UK), the government is responsible for financing social welfare but not necessarily for its provision. A combination of public administrations, nonprofits, and private companies carries out the provision of social welfare. The model encourages competition between them and is structured through private contracts, not subsidies (Hoogendoorn et al., 2010).

The strategies previously described emerged in the 1980s and early 1990s and offered diverse fittings to the type of social enterprise that had taken hold with greater intensity in Europe at that time: Work Integration Social Enterprises (WISE) – In other words, organisations whose mission was to offer jobs to the vulnerable unemployed. However, the expression "social enterprise" wasn't used in Europe until 1990. The first documented mention of it was in Italy, introduced by a newspaper called *Impresa Sociale* (Defourny & Nyssens, 2012).

During the late 1990s and the first part of the twenty-first century, the relevance of social entrepreneurship accelerated in Europe. Social entrepreneurship became a broad notion incorporating elements of the various approaches previously described. At the end of the 1990s, the UK created the Coalition of Social Enterprises and the Social Exclusion Unit, which used the term "social enterprise" to refer to nonprofit organisations and companies created by local communities to promote the inclusion of vulnerable people (Somerville, 2012) very much along the lines of Ireland's Community Enterprise Programme.

In Europe, consistent with the way in which social entrepreneurship developed, academics interested in it initially were mainly those in social sciences such as sociology, economics, or political science. Not so much those in the business management space. Only in the 1990s did some European business schools develop a nascent research interest in social entrepreneurship, influenced by their counterparts in the USA (Kerlin, 2006).

The USA Tradition: Market-Generated Revenue and Innovation for a Social Cause

In the USA, social entrepreneurship was always considered a business school topic academically. From the beginning, it was considered part of the academic area of entrepreneurship within business management research, although it also attracted the attention of academics in the social sciences (Defourny & Nyssens, 2012; Hoogendoorn et al., 2010). This is because the emergence of social entrepreneurship in the USA differs from the European experience in important ways.

Voluntary and charitable nonprofit organisations, often affiliated with religious groups, had traditionally taken care of aiding those in need in the USA. These organisations were typically funded by private donors belonging to the community and partly by government subsidies. In addition, they commonly sold handicrafts or second-hand items in street markets to top up the funding they needed. The development of social enterprises and the popularisation of the term in the USA began in the 1970s when it became more common for these nonprofit organisations to develop strategies to increase the percentage of their income from commercial activities (Galera & Borzaga, 2009; Hoogendoorn et al., 2010).

During the 1990s, the trend for nonprofits to incorporate business management tools and commercial activity grew in the USA (Boschee, 1995). At the same time, the number of entrepreneurs creating companies with a social mission was also growing. These hybrid initiatives between business management and social action initially received multiple names (Defourny & Nyssens, 2012), until the mid-1990s, when the terms "social entrepreneurship," "social entrepreneur," or "social enterprise" began to consolidate in the USA (Defourny & Nyssens, 2010).

But, also in the USA, social entrepreneurship didn't emerge as a monolithic movement. Here too, different schools of thought regarding social entrepreneurship emerged (Anderson & Dees, 2006):

Income generation: Under this paradigm, social enterprises are nonprofit organisations that use commercial activities to finance their social activities (Kerlin, 2006). A whole sector of businesses founded by nonprofits began to develop. These organisations are often called "entrepreneurial nonprofits" and usually combine income streams from commercial activities, grants, and donations.

Social innovation: This school of thought focuses not on social enterprises at the organisational level but on individual entrepreneurs, in the Schumpeterian sense of the word, seeking to transform society by generating social innovation (Anderson & Dees, 2006). One of the most widely cited definitions of social entrepreneurship falls within this notion:

"Social entrepreneurs play the role of change agents in the social sector, by: Adopting a mission to create and sustain social value (not just private value), recognizing and relentlessly pursuing new opportunities to serve that mission, engaging in a process of continuous innovation, adaptation, and learning, acting boldly without being limited by resources currently in hand, and exhibiting a heightened sense of accountability to the constituencies served and for the outcomes created."

(Dees, 1998b, p. 4)

Social Entrepreneurship Nowadays

By the first decade of the twenty first century, social entrepreneurship, social enterprise, and social entrepreneur were already widely known and used in Europe and the USA. However, since these concepts had developed in parallel in both regions, it meant somewhat different things in each region and for different people within each region. In all cases, the common feature of social entrepreneurship was the social purpose of the activity.

In the USA, the two schools of thought have partially merged, and it became common to see that organisations focusing on social innovation would incorporate a market-generated revenue component to support the economic sustainability of the solutions. Conversely, nonprofits that had initially launched a commercial branch solely to boost their revenue began to work on a social innovation edge to their business models.

The European side of the debate underwent a similar process. Social enterprises broadened their scope beyond labour inclusion (Galera & Borzaga, 2009) to promote culture, environmental protection, urban regeneration, and so forth. Market-generated income and innovation in nonprofits became more prevalent across European countries. In the European approach, involving stakeholders and beneficiaries in the organisation's governance structure continues to be important, inspired by the cooperative movement.

The idea of the social economy, as the space encompassing many of these social purpose actors, and in particular those characterised by democratic governance, gained prominence in Europe in practice, policy, and research. As of April 2023, the official definition of social enterprise by the European Commission is the following:

> A social enterprise is an operator in the social economy whose main objective is to have a social impact rather than make a profit for their owners or shareholders. It operates by providing goods and services for the market in an entrepreneurial and innovative fashion and uses its profits primarily to achieve social objectives. It is managed in an open and responsible manner and, in particular, involves employees, consumers and stakeholders affected by its commercial activities.
>
> (European Commission, Social enterprises)

At present, the various approaches have converged in a shared and diverse melting pot. We must point out, though, that in academic research there are different streams of research on social entrepreneurship (associated with the USA approach), social economy (associated with the European approach), and social enterprise (originating in parallel in the USA and Europe). In this book, our grounding concept is social entrepreneurship, but we take the practitioner approach of using the terms more practically, which is the direction of the field. That is not to say that we are ignoring the differences between different approaches. It is important to keep in mind a defining and persistent feature of social entrepreneurship: Its plurality, shaped by the various perspectives and traditions that influence it.

We realise that, up to this point, we have only discussed the traditions of Europe and the USA. This is because the term "social entrepreneurship" mostly emerged there. Nowadays, the term "social entrepreneurship" has been picked up in many other regions, where it takes on unique and diverse characteristics influenced by socio-economic, cultural, and contextual factors. For example, the African continent presents a unique ground for social entrepreneurs (Ashoka Africa, 2023; Rivera-Santos et al., 2015). In the region, as in other developing contexts, personal experiences have a profound impact on social entrepreneurs, driving them to engage in solutions to issues they've experienced firsthand (Wanyoike & Maseno, 2021). Initiatives aimed at fostering social entrepreneurship in Africa are continually evolving despite the challenges (Kabbaj et al., 2016). The same could be said about Asia or Latin America. Their unique contexts have shaped the strategies and missions of its social entrepreneurs.

In addition, you might be thinking: Throughout the whole chapter, there has been no mention of the environment! These authors do not know what world we are living in! You see, it's important to note that in the past, unfortunately, environmental issues simply weren't in the spotlight. This has changed. Today, we're witnessing growing numbers of social entrepreneurs who are taking on environmental challenges alongside their social missions. So, while this book's historical perspective may not emphasise environmental aspects, it's crucial to understand that social entrepreneurship is evolving to address these urgent environmental issues, as described in the introduction of the book. This is not to say that there weren't social entrepreneurs 15 or 20 years ago who focused on environmental matters, but they weren't the majority. Here's to them!

Problem Solved! . . . Right?

So, we've just said that all the different approaches to social entrepreneurship have converged in a shared and diverse melting pot, expanding across the world and adding an environmental lens to the social one. Kudos! Right? Well, let's not get ahead of ourselves.

Imagine you deeply care about solving a social/environmental issue and have created a social enterprise to tackle it. Actually, if you have chosen this book, you may very well be in that exact situation. Before reading this first chapter, had you checked the European Commission's official definition of social entrepreneurship? Had you read Dees' definition? Had you spent time wondering about the exact definition at all? Most people don't. They are way too busy trying to solve an important problem facing humanity and/or the planet.

The closest that most social entrepreneurs get to looking at formal definitions is going through the specific requirements to apply for one social entrepreneurship award or another. And, then, the main focus is usually not on whether a given organisation's checklist is the best depiction of what a social enterprise is. The focus is on whether applying is a good use of my time based on the realistic chances of being selected and the money and support I might get if I am.

For example, imagine you consider yourself a social entrepreneur and your social enterprise is registered as a nonprofit. If the checklist of requirements of a specific social entrepreneurship fellowship programme says that you must have a profit-distributing business model to be selected, you simply don't apply. And that's it. You move on to the website of another organisation whose requirements you do fit. Usually, you aren't left with a terrible identity crisis, confused and not knowing if you are indeed a social entrepreneur or not. After all, you were looking for resources; you weren't looking for a definition and, most likely, didn't feel you needed one. But then, why did you think you were a social entrepreneur in the first place?

In practice, people do not read definitions and choose an approach from the various definitions before putting together their projects. Rather, they engage in an organic discovery process. They may first find a problem they want to solve, envision a solution, and try to implement it. At some point in that process, they might hear from someone around them that there is such a thing as social entrepreneurship. "Why don't you apply to this programme for social enterprises?" "Social enterprises? Sounds good. Yes, I might apply." Or, they attend a conference where this expression is used. Or they may know the expression from before, having worked in a context, be it third sector or startups, where the term was used. The list of ways people run into the notion of social entrepreneurship and self-identify as a social entrepreneur is long. Of all of them, the one in which they will have gone through a formal definition is if they had heard about it at school where a professor, like us, will have forced them to go through the pain we've just put you through in this chapter. But, even then, unless they went through the course already thinking about creating a social enterprise (knowing that you will use the knowledge always increases attention levels), it might not have been the most engaging and memorable session of all.

Okay, and what about all those people from whom our imaginary social entrepreneur has heard the expression, and who collectively have led this person to consider the project a social enterprise: Have they been reading definitions? By now, you have already guessed they probably have not. They learned about social entrepreneurship in the same way, by hearing it organically from other people. All of them have grown academically and professionally within a given tradition, and they will assign words a meaning consistent with that tradition. This leaves us with a plural, and fragmented, social enterprise ecosystem.

If you have attended business school, you might think social entrepreneurship is first and foremost about founding a startup, with all the values that business schools typically attach to that word, including profitability and high growth. But if you have learned about social entrepreneurship from someone who considers that a social entrepreneur (the individual) is first and foremost a changemaker (the social innovation paradigm previously described), you might have even heard that having a profit-oriented model is a problem and you should avoid it. Or maybe not. Depending on how close this person is to the income generation stream. If you graduated from sociology or have studied economic development, you probably ran into social entrepreneurship as a way to organise to solve social problems from someone who didn't place much importance on the funding model. If you have grown professionally in a space connected to cooperatives (maybe in Europe but maybe elsewhere, like Latin America), governance and stakeholder participation might be critical for you.

Aren't we beyond all of this? No. Long-standing historic traditions die hard. Social entrepreneurship is not, and might never become, a monolithic reality. It might not even be desirable for it to be more specific than it is. In practice, nowadays, social entrepreneurship looks like a combination of various approaches, focusing first and foremost on solving a social/environmental problem in a new/innovative way and with varying considerations for funding strategies and governance structures.

Box 1.1   João Magalhães, Code For All

Being a social entrepreneur is not a matter of what legal framework you use or if you are for-profit or nonprofit. It's more about having it in your DNA. How can we scale a social innovation? And how can we impact real people's lives? That's it. That's my definition.

Conclusion

To sum it up, in this chapter we explored how the concept of social entrepreneurship took shape, initially in Europe and the USA. These approaches converged in a shared and diverse melting pot, expanding globally, adding different perspectives in the various regions in which it expanded and incorporating an environmental lens. Acknowledging the plurality of social entrepreneurship, influenced by diverse perspectives and traditions, is critical.

The variety of approaches, shaped by academic and professional traditions, remains a constant. People and organisations jump into the concept in their own way without always sticking to formal definitions. Let's appreciate the diversity and recognise that social entrepreneurship is this ever-changing, always interesting journey.

References

Anderson, B. B., & Dees, J. G. (2006). Rhetoric, reality, and research: Building a solid foundation for the practice of social entrepreneurship. *Social Entrepreneurship: New Models of Sustainable Social Change*, 144–168.

Ashoka Africa. (2023, July). *Roots of change: How social entrepreneurs advance systems change in Africa*. Ashoka. www.ashoka.org/en-aaw/roots-of-change

Austin, J., Stevenson, H., & Wei-Skillern, J. (2006). Social and commercial entrepreneurship: Same, different, or both? *Entrepreneurship Theory and Practice, 30*(1), 1–22.

Bacq, S., & Janssen, F. (2011). The multiple faces of social entrepreneurship: A review of definitional issues based on geographical and thematic criteria. *Entrepreneurship & Regional Development, 23*(5–6), 373–403.

Bornstein, D. (2007). *How to change the world: Social entrepreneurs and the power of new ideas*. Oxford University Press.

Boschee, J. (1995). Some nonprofits are not only thinking about the unthinkable, they're doing it – running a profit. *Across the Board, the Conference Board Magazine, 32*(3), 20–25.

Dearlove, D. (2004). Interview: Jeff Skoll. *Business Strategy Review, 15*(2), 51–53.

Dees, J. G. (1998a). Enterprising nonprofits. *Harvard Business Review, 76*(1), 54–67.

Dees, J. G. (1998b). *The meaning of social entrepreneurship* (p. 6). Comments and Suggestions Contributed from the Social Entrepreneurship

Funders Working Group, Draft Report for the Kauffman Center for Entrepreneurial Leadership.

Defourny, J., & Nyssens, M. (2010). Conceptions of social enterprise and social entrepreneurship in Europe and the United States: Convergences and divergences. *Journal of Social Entrepreneurship, 1*(1), 32–53.

Defourny, J., & Nyssens, M. (2012). El enfoque EMES de empresa social desde una perspectiva comparada. *CIRIEC-España, Revista de Economía Pública, Social y Cooperativa, 75*, 6–34.

Defourny, J., & Nyssens, M. (2017). Fundamentals for an international typology of social enterprise models. *VOLUNTAS: International Journal of Voluntary and Nonprofit Organizations, 28*, 2469–2497.

European Commission, Social enterprises, https://single-market-economy. ec.europa.eu/sectors/proximity-and-social-economy/social-economy-eu/social-enterprises_en#:~:text=A%20social%20enterprise%20is%20 an,for%20their%20owners%20or%20shareholders.

Galera, G., & Borzaga, C. (2009). Social enterprise. *Social Enterprise Journal, 5*(3), 210–228.

Hoogendoorn, B., Pennings, E., & Thurik, R. (2010). What do we know about social entrepreneurship: An analysis of empirical research. *International Review of Entrepreneurship, 8*(2).

Kabbaj, M., El Ouazzani Ech Hadi, K. H. A. L. I. D., Elamrani, J., & Lemtaoui, M. (2016). A study of the social entrepreneurship ecosystem: The case of Morocco. *Journal of Developmental Entrepreneurship, 21*(4), 1650021.

Kerlin, J. A. (2006). Social enterprise in the United States and Europe: Understanding and learning from the differences. *VOLUNTAS: International Journal of Voluntary and Nonprofit Organizations, 17*, 246–262.

Martin, R. L., & Osberg, S. (2007). Social entrepreneurship: the case for definition. *Stanford Social Innovation Review, 5*(2), 28–39.

Nicholls, A. (2006). *Social entrepreneurship: New models of sustainable social change*. Oxford University Press.

O'Hara, P. (2001). Ireland: Social enterprises and local development. In *The emergence of social enterprise* (pp. 161–177). Routledge.

Rivera-Santos, M., Holt, D., Littlewood, D., & Kolk, A. (2015). Social entrepreneurship in sub-Saharan Africa. *The Academy of Management Perspective, 29*(1), 72–91.

Roberts, D. & Woods, C. (2005). Changing the world on a shoestring: The concept of social entrepreneurship. *University of Auckland Business Review, 7*(1), 45–51.

Santos, F. M. (2012). A positive theory of social entrepreneurship. *Journal of Business Ethics, 111*(3), 335–351.

Somerville, P. (2012). *Social relations and social exclusion: Rethinking political economy*. Routledge.

Wanyoike, C. N., & Maseno, M. (2021). Exploring the motivation of social entrepreneurs in creating successful social enterprises in East Africa. *New England Journal of Entrepreneurship, 24*(2), 79–104.

Weerawardena, J., & Mort, G. S. (2006). Investigating social entrepreneurship: A multidimensional model. *Journal of World Business, 41*(1), 21–35.

Welsh, D. H. B. (2012). The evolution of social entrepreneurship: What have we learned? *Journal of Technology Management in China, 7*(3), 270–290.

Young, D. R. (2013). *If not for profit, for what?* (1983 Print ed.). Lexington Books.

2   How Every Sector Got So Excited about Social Enterprise

The Four Failure Theory

Underpinning much of the practice and research of social entrepreneurship is a normative assumption that it is good. While some studies are explicit about social entrepreneurship having positive impacts (Santos, 2012), most take its legitimacy as a better way of organising for granted (Dart, 2004). This improvement refers to positive social or environmental impacts, which social enterprises, by definition, must balance with financial goals, be they for profit or not. Are we about to say that social entrepreneurship is **not** a better way of organising for positive impact? Don't drop the book too soon, social entrepreneurship fan. All we are saying so far is that it is an aspirational term, full of promise. As a result, both for-profit companies and nonprofit organisations can benefit from identifying as a social enterprise, which is why the concept is so popular. And since most countries have no specific legal form of social enterprise, it remains a descriptive term. Actually, self-descriptive in most cases. Sure, it may be defined in policy, but as long as there is no legal form, definitions are open to interpretation. And the definitional debate is a hot one, as we saw in the previous chapter. By the way, as you will learn later in the book, we don't necessarily support the notion that there should be one legal form to depict all social enterprises – that would damage the diversity of the ecosystem.

The normative aspect of social enterprise is reflected in the rapid growth and expansion of the practice and research on the topic, which is described as a "big tent" approach, meaning that the concept can include a wide diverse array of ideas and definitions (Martin & Osberg, 2007; Nicholls, 2010). Simply put, many are jumping on the social enterprise bandwagon. Social enterprise as organisational type(s) and social entrepreneurship as a practice has swept across the world and is found on every continent. This enthusiasm is actually part of the challenge of social entrepreneurship, as expectations are impossibly high and social change timeframes are underestimated (see Part 2). Researchers have gained an understanding of how different socio-economic institutional contexts shape expressions of social enterprise (Kerlin, 2013), as well as an understanding of the range of different types of social entrepreneurial forms and their prevalence across the world (Defourny et al., 2020).

DOI: 10.4324/9781003409694-4

But how specifically does social entrepreneurship represent improvement? To answer that question, we build on the idea of three sectors and develop the Four Failure Theory of Social Entrepreneurship

The three sectors are: Public (government), business (for-profit), and community (nonprofit or civil society). How these sectors organise differs between countries and is shaped by history and policy, but the concept of three sectors has shaped different approaches to organising. Social entrepreneurship can be understood as the blurring of boundaries between the sectors (a space sometimes referred to as a fourth sector), so diving a little deeper into them is helpful. The Four Failure Theory of Social Entrepreneurship is that the emergence and rise of social entrepreneurship is due to the limitations, or perceived failures, of each of the three sectors, and of the sector model in general.

The three failure theory explains the roles of the three sectors, as filling the gaps left by the other two sectors (Steinberg, 2006). It is a macro-economic theory suggesting that the three sectors are in competition with each other, vying to fulfil unmet needs and demands for services and products.

- The first sector, public, exists to provide policies, laws, and services for the common good. The kinds of services public sectors traditionally provide are those that all members of society benefit from – roads, electricity, water, healthcare, education, and social welfare support. The "failure" of the first sector is that governments tend not to take risks with public funding, which prevents them from innovating to create new products and services. The public sector is supposed to be driven by responsibility to the broad citizenship (not niche services for the few) and transparency (not risk-taking).
- In contrast, the second sector is made up of private, profit-making companies that excel at innovation and risk-taking, competition, and selling products, creating new markets for services and goods that people are willing to pay for. As well as tapping into the mass markets, the for-profit sector is also excellent at providing niche services that benefit a subset of society, from acupuncture to leadership training. The "failure" of the second sector is that when services require trust, such as childcare or elderly care, users are less likely to rely on a profit-maximisation approach (called, contract-failure). Or, when there simply isn't a profit motivation, like a membership club, the for-profit firm falls short. Those areas are where the third sector steps in.
- The third, or nonprofit sector, provides services that benefit the public that the state does not provide, often when the beneficiaries are a small group or have historically established a relationship with that subset of society. The third sector has many different types of organisations – associations, foundations, nonprofits, NGOs, societies, and clubs – and includes all the various ways that civil society organises to meet its own needs. It excels at

organising when trust is essential, and when there is no great profit motive, like a community or hobby group. The third sector "fails" to provide general public services and "fails" to drive economic growth. That is where the first and second sectors step in.

The three sectors help explain the different ways that social entrepreneurship is seen as an improvement on previous ways of organising. To be clear, this chapter doesn't try to prove that the general concept of social entrepreneurship represents an improvement to the general three-sector model; no data set could prove that general statement. What we are concerned with is providing an explanation for the huge enthusiasm for social entrepreneurship. This enthusiasm has fuelled the emergence and growth of social entrepreneurship, is often acknowledged by social entrepreneurs, and has led to some of the pitfalls that we cover in Part 2.

Improved First Sector: Social Enterprises Providing Employment as Part of Social Welfare

While the first sector is primary in providing social welfare, policies in the 1990s shifted to providing employment as part of social welfare provision. The policy of providing supported employment to marginalised people gave rise to Work Integrated Social Enterprises (WISE) in Europe and elsewhere. Also called Public Social Enterprises, these organisations were seen as an improvement to previous approaches where social welfare recipients fell into the poverty trap, becoming dependent on social welfare and unable to progress out of that dependency. The idea was that social enterprise employment was empowering, whereas social welfare support could sometimes become disempowering. Thus, social entrepreneurship can be a "better" way of providing social welfare, or an improvement of the first sector.

Improved Second Sector: Social Enterprises as Prosocial, Green Businesses

The second sector has been reacting to two big accusations over the past few decades: Its role in increasing socio-economic inequality, and its negative impact on the natural environment. In response to the first accusation, some businesses have made efforts to become more "social." They sign up to Fairtrade, include a wider group of stakeholders in their strategies and plans, or increase their community engagement, among other strategies. In response to the second accusation, they are trying to become more "green" by becoming carbon neutral, making their products recyclable, or by implementing environmental innovations, for example. These trends are consistent with the rise of Social Businesses. However, unlike the normal businesses that strive to be responsible or sustainable, which we just described, the Social Business approach to social entrepreneurship consists of for-profit, second-sector companies that exist first and foremost to advance a social or environmental mission. They incorporate as for-profit because, due to their impact model, they find that to be the best way to advance their mission. But their business model is a means to an impact-end, never an end in itself.

During the eighteenth century, in the private sector, the idea that the labourers should benefit from the profit of the company gave rise to the cooperative business form, where the labourers are also the shareholders. The cooperative movement was partly a reaction to labour exploitation and economic inequality and offered an alternative to the conventional system of organising in open markets (Ridley-Duff, 2019). The democratic governance principles of social cooperatives ensure that the profit derived from the labour of a business is distributed among its members. Based on the traditional cooperative form, Social Cooperatives emerged. Social Cooperatives differ from Social Business, which does not challenge the system in which businesses operate at such a fundamental level. Thus, they represent different perspectives and traditions on improvement of the second sector that cut across the political spectrum in different ways in different countries.

Improved Third Sector: Social Enterprises as Entrepreneurial Nonprofits

While the third sector has a wide range of organisational forms that differ between countries, a common feature is that these organisations depend on donations from individuals or philanthropic bodies or grants from government or private agencies. Some nonprofits are themselves grant-giving, such as philanthropic foundations. Nonprofit organisations usually are not separate legal forms, but are assigned legal designations (e.g. charity, association) regulated by policy, differing in each country depending on the legal framework. The perceived improvement from charity to social enterprise is a move from being donor-dependent to having generated revenue and/or being more innovative. Donor funding, particularly in the form of grants, requires writing detailed grant applications, is tied to specific activities, and demands detailed reporting. While it is important that public funding is tightly accounted for, these practices use up precious time in nonprofits, and often prevent innovation, as "restricted" funding cannot accommodate for adapting to changing circumstances very easily. Income generated through sales or service provision is "unrestricted," meaning that, like a for-profit business, the manager or entrepreneur has more flexibility allocating the usually tight budget. Thus, an organisation can be more innovative and adaptive when it has generated revenue. In the third sector, therefore, we have the social enterprise type: Entrepreneurial nonprofit, which is seen as "better" than traditional charity.

Different Social Enterprise Types

Building on the three failure economic theory, we propose that different types of social enterprises emerged in response to a perceived failure within the sector model; this represents three of the four failures in the emergence of social entrepreneurship. The Public Social Enterprise type reflects the failure of social welfare to address poverty and other public needs adequately. The Social Business type reflects the failure of businesses. The social-environmental-financial balance that social enterprises boast contrasts with the failures of traditional profit-making businesses, which are blamed for their role in, and inadequate responses to, environmental degradation and socio-economic inequality (Dyllick & Muff, 2015; Kramer et al., 2019). The Social Cooperative type reflects the failure of traditional businesses to fairly share value between stakeholders. The Entrepreneurial Nonprofit type reflects the failure of the third sector to effectively and efficiently scale good ideas as they are limited by donations. These four types of social enterprises have been identified and examined by researchers, who found that the Public Social Enterprise type is actually more like a subset of the Entrepreneurial Nonprofit (Defourny et al., 2020). Table 2.1 illustrates the four types with examples that you will find in this book.

The Fourth Failure: The Sector Model

So far, in this chapter, we have mostly focused on forms of social enterprising at an organisational level. But, as discussed in the previous chapter, there is also the social innovation approach to social entrepreneurship, which aspires

Table 2.1 Social enterprise types as improvements on sectoral failures

Social enterprise type	Sector failure	Examples included in this book
Public Social Enterprise	Failure of governments to provide social welfare that empowered people to move out of poverty.	Shuttle Knit Fundación Juanfe Recode
Social Business	Failure of businesses to address socio-economic inequality and environmental degradation.	Moyee Coffee Article 22 Code for All NaviLens
Social Cooperative	Failure of businesses to share profit fairly with the labourers.	Phu Quy Agricultural Farm Joint Stock Company
Entrepreneurial Nonprofit	Failure of nonprofits to be innovative and adequately address social challenges.	Proudly Made in Africa COBATI

to transcend the limitations of the traditional three sectors. The social innovation approach zeroes in on individual entrepreneurs in the Schumpeterian sense. These innovative individuals, acting as catalysts of change, seek to transform society through the generation of social innovation. They recognise that addressing these challenges often requires fresh, unconventional ideas that don't neatly fit into traditional sectors. By emphasising individual agency and innovation, the social innovation approach effectively speaks to the various shortcomings of the public, for-profit, and nonprofit sectors. In summary, the innovative individual approach to social entrepreneurship is a response to limitations, or "failures," in all three sectors, and in the sector model in general, that new ideas are needed to solve social and environmental challenges that are not boxed into sectors. Thus, these four failures of the three sectors and of the sector model help to explain how and why social entrepreneurship emerged and exists and why it is seen as an improvement on older forms of organising for social/environmental purpose. This perceived improvement contributes to the high expectations associated with social entrepreneurship that are not always helpful.

Box 2.1   Killian Stokes, Moyee Coffee

When I went to Uganda in 2008 I saw farmers who were working so hard and earning so little. And I thought, why are we giving these people charity when they grow such fabulous coffee? That was my lightbulb moment. I went, hang on, business is not serving these stakeholders. So we're having to come in and grant aid it, with a government programme. So I realised, this is not rocket science; we can solve this with business. That led me on a journey to explore value chains. It was not about aid or sending kids to school; it wasn't about education or charity; it was literally looking at jobs. Why are these people working 40 hours a week and not earning enough, and they're growing a product that the world wants? The economy is not working for these farmers.

   Those mountainous farming regions in Kenya have tea and coffee growing on them. What doesn't help is if a living income for people in that part of the world is 1500 USD per year and they're only earning 400. That's the price of the tea or coffee they're getting. So I started an ethical coffee business in 2016. Part of my motivation was that I wanted a job for myself and I didn't want to work for the NGOs. I was burnt out working for charities. And I was having questions around the impact of traditional charities. They can be quite bureaucratic whereas I knew that business tended to be more open to innovation. You could actually do stuff and get feedback, get a return on your investment. That was an appeal for me.

International Development and Social Entrepreneurship

Social entrepreneurship is also seen as an improvement on development aid. As mentioned above, national legal frameworks for starting up a business or a nonprofit will shape and influence the options available to social entrepreneurs in any given country. In addition to that, national-institutional contexts – meaning the social, cultural, historical, and economic features – influence how social entrepreneurship has evolved in different countries (Kerlin, 2013).

In countries that have large welfare states and strong economies, you are likely to find public funding for social entrepreneurship, or at least for some of its forms (most European countries). In countries that have less social welfare, you are likely to find a diverse array of autonomous social enterprises and more examples of the Social Business type (United Kingdom (UK), United States (USA), and developing countries). In countries with weaker governments and economies that are in receipt of development aid, we mostly find international funding for entrepreneurial nonprofits and social businesses that take a "trade not aid" approach. This is characterised by the normative assumption that social entrepreneurship is an improvement on previous forms of aid, similar to the Four Failure Theory above.

Box 2.2   Maria Baryamujura, COBATI

Uganda's main newspaper did an article on me. Thanks to it, I got the attention of the Country Representative of UNDP – United Nations Development Program – and he supported me to begin growing my idea of using tourism as a tool for community empowerment and rural transformation.

In response to criticism of international development aid, state and institutional donors are turning to support entrepreneurial initiatives for communities, so that they can develop more sustainable sources of funding, and not remain reliant on grant aid long term. In particular, countries like Viet Nam that are moving out of the "less developed" country status as their economy gets stronger, international aid is winding down, so strategies look to support self-sustaining initiatives, such as entrepreneurial community businesses (Truong et al., 2019). Similarly, entrepreneurs in Europe and Africa are looking to business to support development – trade justice rather than aid. For example, Proudly Made in Africa applies the concept of social entrepreneurship in a unique way; they are not one business trying to address a social issue, they are actually a charity promoting trade justice, supporting African businesses to deliver sustainable development in Africa. They are an entrepreneurial nonprofit, reflecting an "improved" approach to third sector organising, but also they are promoting trade justice, a new way and improved way for businesses to address a social issue.

Box 2.3   David Nyaluke, Proudly Made in Africa

The mission from the beginning has been to open market access for products that are made in Africa, supporting entrepreneurs in Africa who have high-quality products to be able to find a market and sell those products in wider markets. . . . Trade justice is replacing development as the way to support African countries' economic development. They thought that the best way to help African countries was with development; traditionally there has been a lot of emphasis on aid, with great generosity towards African and other less developed countries. But now this model is critiqued, and we know that the best way to help African countries in terms of development will be to change the way we let these African countries trade with and be in business with wealthier countries.

We find that African countries have been producers of raw material to other markets. They don't add value to the local area, so most of the value of what they have in the global market are those raw materials. They don't fetch a lot of money to be able to support development. So, the best way to help that transition is to support people to manufacture high-quality products in Africa. But the main thing is that once they have the manufactured products, is to support them to find access to the markets here in Europe and other markets.

Conclusion

This chapter has illustrated all the various ways that social entrepreneurship and social enterprises are seen as an improvement on previous ways of organising. We explain this improvement as the Four Failure Theory of Social Entrepreneurship. The positivity around social entrepreneurship has helped unleash innovative ways of driving positive change, and, on the other hand, this enthusiasm has also brought challenges on which we elaborate in subsequent chapters. But don't worry, the story isn't all bleak, not at all. It is well-founded to be enthusiastic about social entrepreneurship. We definitely are! But now we (collectively, in the "fourth sector") are armed with experience and data to combine with our passion and overcome those challenges.

References

Dart, R. (2004). The legitimacy of social enterprise. *Nonprofit Management and Leadership, 14*(4), 411–424. https://doi.org/10.1002/nml.43

Defourny, J., Nyssens, M., & Brolis, O. (2020). Testing social enterprise models across the world: Evidence from the "international comparative social enterprise models (ICSEM) project." *Nonprofit and Voluntary Sector Quarterly*, online first, 1–21. https://doi.org/10.1177/0899764020959470

Dyllick, T., & Muff, K. (2015). Clarifying the meaning of sustainable business: Introducing a typology from business-as-usual to true business sustainability. *Organization & Environment, 29*(2), 156–174. https://doi.org/10.1177/1086026615575176

Kerlin, J. A. (2013). Defining social enterprise across different contexts: A conceptual framework based on institutional factors. *Nonprofit and Voluntary Sector Quarterly, 42*(1), 84–108. https://doi.org/10.1177/0899764011433040

Kramer, M. R., Agarwal, R., & Srinivas, A. (2019). Business as usual will not save the planet. *Harvard Business Review*. https://hbr.org/2019/06/business-as-usual-will-not-save-the-planet

Martin, R. L., & Osberg, S. (2007, Spring). Social entrepreneurship: The case for definition. *Stanford Social Innovation Review*, 28–39.

Nicholls, A. (2010). The legitimacy of social entrepreneurship: Reflexive isomorphism in a pre-paradigmatic field. *Entrepreneurship Theory and Practice, 34*(4), 611–633. https://doi.org/10.1111/j.1540-6520.2010.00397.x

Ridley-Duff, R. (2019). *Understanding social enterprise: Theory and practice* (3rd ed.). Sage Publishing.

Santos, F. M. (2012). A positive theory of social entrepreneurship. *Journal of Business Ethics, 111*(3), 335–351. ABI/INFORM Global; Social Science Premium Collection. https://doi.org/10.1007/s10551-012-1413-4

Steinberg, R. (2006). Economic theories of nonprofit organizations. In *The nonprofit sector: A research handbook* (pp. 117–139). Yale University Press.

Truong, T. T. N., Cannon, S. M., Picton, C., Sareen, S., & Rhodes, M. L. (2019). *Social enterprises in Viet Nam and Ireland*. Labor Publishing House (Nha xuat ban lao động).

3   Levers of Positive Change

In Chapter 1 we reviewed the historical emergence of the different traditions and approaches to social entrepreneurship, while in Chapter 2 we provided a theoretical explanation for that emergence and growth around the world. What is remarkable and fascinating is that the many different approaches to social entrepreneurship grew in parallel in so many places. It appears that there was/is an appetite globally to engage with organising to improve our communities and protect the environment in a different way. More and more people are engaging with social/environmental purpose initiatives in innovative ways and trying to make the world a better place. When you stop and think about it, this is quite amazing. After the awe subsides (take a deep breath), we can unpack that positive global surge; we find four key elements that work as levers of positive change, presented below.

Unveiling the Distinctive Traits of Social Entrepreneurs

Social entrepreneurs tend to show some unique qualities that really catch our eye. They make them different from your traditional entrepreneurs. Driven by a deep passion, they have a strong desire to tackle important social and environmental problems in new and creative ways. In this section, we're going to take a closer look at what sets these social entrepreneurs apart from the rest:

• Innovation and Creativity: Social entrepreneurs are innovative problem-solvers. They are known for their ability to offer creative solutions to address societal or environmental challenges. They develop new programmes, initiatives, organisations, and products to drive change (Mair & Marti, 2006; Shaw & Carter, 2007).

Box 3.1   Maria Baryamujura, COBATI

I do what I do because of what my life has been like. At a young age I learned of the power of a woman having education and her own

---

DOI: 10.4324/9781003409694-5

money. My parents were both teachers, and my mum was the first woman in her family to get an education. In retirement they practiced mixed farming, and my mum worked hard. She was very talented with her hands, made various crafts for sale, produced food for home and income generation. She always had her own money! So she could afford to give us extra pocket money.

Later, being a young woman, my husband was killed the day before our younger baby was born. I was left with two children. I was devastated, but I had an education and my mother had been a good role model. I worked hard and could take charge of my family. After working in tourism for some years, I learned about the great potential of community tourism and how it helps women be economically independent. This made total sense to me. I saw how all these buses of tourists pass by the communities and the ordinary people are left looking at the bus drive by and not benefit, yet they had the potential to tap into their culture, indigenous knowledge, and countryside green environment to participate and benefit through community tourism-related enterprises. So, in 2001 I registered my nonprofit COBATI – Community Based Tourism Initiative – to change the status quo.

- Collaboration and Team Leadership: Social entrepreneurs are collaborative pioneers who effectively bring together diverse stakeholders to work collectively towards social change and environmental protection. They excel at building and managing teams to drive mission-based performance (Raith & Starke, 2017; Makhlouf, 2011).
- Empathy and Compassion: Empathy is a central quality that fuels social entrepreneurs. They deeply understand the challenges faced by those they aim to serve and are driven by a profound sense of compassion (Glaveli & Geormas, 2018; Koe Hwee Nga & Shamuganathan, 2010).

Box 3.2   Catalina Escobar, Fundación Juanfe

I'm fascinated by numbers. For me, numbers have an incredible logic. But that's what I thought until I was faced with the human side, and I realised that you must consider both. The Juanfe model was not invented by me; it was inspired by the souls of the people in the communities. And when replicating the model, we have seen the same feeling of the Chilean girl, also in the woman from Venezuela. We have a model that works because they are our teachers. We are simply the most effective conduit to translate that in a model that others can understand.

- Altruism: Social entrepreneurs are primarily motivated by creating social and environmental value rather than financial gain. They have a strong sense of responsibility and are driven by a desire to make a positive difference (Santos, 2012; Bornstein, 2004).
- Resilience and Adaptability in Overcoming Challenges: Social entrepreneurs often have firsthand experience dealing with the problems they set themselves to confront and are adept at navigating resource constraints. Their resilience in the face of adversity is a defining characteristic (Di Domenico et al., 2010).

Box 3.3   Javier Pita, NaviLens

I don't distinguish much between my activity and my life. When you embark on a project like this, you give it all you have. And in the end, there are always personal stories. I have a brother with Down syndrome, and I have lived with him through the difficulties he has had during his life. And you never detach yourself from these experiences. I think that social entrepreneurs do not differentiate their life or their mission from their enterprise as much as maybe classic commercial entrepreneurs can distinguish both.

- Risk-Taking and Independence: Social entrepreneurs exhibit a propensity for risk-taking and a strong need for independence in pursuing their initiatives (Smith et al., 2014; Mair & Marti, 2006).
- Visionary and Inspirational Leadership: Social entrepreneurs inspire internal and external stakeholders by creating a vision for positive change. Their passionate commitment gains the trust and support needed to drive their missions (Estrin et al., 2013; Martin & Osberg, 2007).
- Proactivity and Persistence: As proactive problem-solvers, social entrepreneurs possess entrepreneurial competencies, including initiative, commitment, persuasion, networking, and persistence. These qualities empower them to address challenges effectively (Dey & Steyaert, 2016; Smith et al., 2014).
- Global Exposure and Education: Social entrepreneurs often have a well-rounded education and exposure to global issues. They draw from their diverse experiences to inform their initiatives (Pangriya, 2019; Aileen Boluk & Mottiar, 2014).
- Self-Transcendence and Contentment: Driven by impact, social entrepreneurs transcend self-interest and prioritise positively impacting society. They derive personal satisfaction from benefiting others and are content with the fulfilment of their mission (Pangriya, 2019; Vasakarla, 2008).

Box 3.4   João Magalhães, Code For All

I had a typical career in finance and strategy and an MBA so then shift-ing to becoming a social entrepreneur was kind of a shock. I found the work I did very interesting, but I was always feeling that something was missing. When there was this opportunity of building and creating a social enterprise, everything made much more sense. Having impact in real people's lives, that was the most inspiring thing.

As we conclude this exploration of the heroic traits that define social entre-preneurs, are you not enamoured with their exceptional qualities? Sure thing! They are the ultimate changemakers, top-of-the-range trailblazers equipped with innovation, empathy, and an unwavering commitment to the greater good. But, as we'll soon discuss, every hero has their vulnerabilities, and painting them as flawless saviours is a narrative worth questioning. In our next chapter, we'll pull back the curtain to reveal the complexities and vulnerabili-ties that make the story of social entrepreneurs all the more intriguing. Stay tuned for the unravelling of the extraordinary human journey behind these heroic endeavours.

Unlocking the Power of Social Impact Measurement

In the realm of social entrepreneurship, a resounding drumbeat has emerged – the call for understanding and quantifying social impact. The clarion call to measure social impact comes with good reason, for it embodies the qualities of effectiveness, efficiency, and transparency. But before we dive into contem-porary practices, let's take a look at the rich tapestry from which the practice of social impact measurement has evolved.

Two Traditions: Business and Philanthropy: The roots of social impact measurement run deep, branching out from two distinct traditions. The first traces back to the early days of management science, where Howard R. Bow-en's work in 1953 heralded a new era of considering the social performance of businesses. This tradition gave rise to the practice of Social Accounting and Audit, where companies began to measure both financial and non-financial impact (Gray, 2000). The concept of the "triple bottom line," encompassing social, environmental, and financial aspects, emerged as a beacon in this tra-dition, shaping the modern practice of reporting Environmental, Social, and Governance (ESG) factors.

Building upon this legacy, modern social enterprises often adopt the monetisation of social impact, aiming to convert their noble missions into quantifiable results. The financial quantification of social impact introduces a new dimension that resonates with impact investors and government contractors, who seek tangible evidence of value delivered.

The second tradition hails from the world of nonprofit organisations and philanthropy. Here, the focus is on social impact assessment, emphasising transparency upwards to donors and downwards to beneficiaries (Dufour, 2015; Costa & Andreaus, 2021). The goal is to measure how well an organisation is fulfilling its social mission, a process rooted in the heart of philanthropic endeavours.

Over the years, this tradition has given rise to numerous tools and methods for measuring impact, often structured around the impact value chain also known as the Theory of Change, which lays out the steps from activities to outputs, outcomes, and ultimately impact (McLoughlin et al., 2009; Kah & Akenroye, 2020). Social impact assessment, within this tradition, is closely aligned with the organisation's purpose and its success in realising its intended mission.

Navigating the Diverse Landscape of Impact Measurement: Despite the rich traditions and evolving practices, one common thread emerges – the quest for effective measurement of social impact. Researchers and practitioners have found that the important feature of any method or framework is that it is a good fit with the organisation, considering enterprise size, purpose, specific context, and reason for measuring impact (Rawhouser et al., 2019). The utility of these methodologies has been a subject of exploration, with some findings suggesting that complex and resource-intensive quantitative methods, such as Social Return on Investment (SROI), may win you credibility in the eyes of donors, but may also hold less value for practitioners (Luke et al., 2013). Qualitative assessments that align closely with specific organisational objectives have often been deemed more beneficial (Costa & Andreaus, 2021).

Box 3.5   Rodrigo Baggio, Recode

As a social entrepreneur, people trust in you and your organisation. We need to perform very well in governance and transparency. We need more than being ethical; we need to promote and show how ethical we are. So, measuring impact is very important. We do it using technology systems to collect data and then analyse and produce reports for our sponsors and society. We keep an external audit and have a financial committee reviewing our books. Creating the system to show the numbers in ways that people understand is challenging. Often numbers don't offer a complete picture. You need to do videos and other content to convey the impact.

The Promise of Social Impact Measurement: The allure of social impact measurement extends beyond accountability; it opens new doors to funding sources, particularly from impact investors. Establishing and signalling legitimacy to key stakeholders, as observed by multiple studies, can be a transformative aspect of social impact measurement (Luke et al., 2013; Haski-Leventhal & Mehra, 2016). Social enterprises can leverage this newfound legitimacy to enhance their strategic planning and organisational learning processes (Lall, 2019).

Box 3.6   Catalina Escobar, Fundación Juanfe

I read about Randomized Control Trials (RCT) and took a plane to Boston, to the MIT Poverty Action Lab, JPal. We already did surveys and knew that Juanfe changed the lives of the girls and had a relevant social impact. But measuring the impact rigorously with RCT was expensive. The Inter-American Development Bank supported us, and now we have a proven impact that allows us to grow without being questioned.

Nevertheless, like any burgeoning field, social impact measurement is not without its limitations. Some studies (e.g. Ruebottom, 2011) raise concerns about an overemphasis on measuring performance and advocate for a broader approach to social change that may better suit the purpose and character of many social enterprises. As stated earlier, it's a question of fit.

As we move forward, it's essential to recognise that social impact measurement is an evolving art and/or science that integrates insights from both business and philanthropy traditions. It is a tool for empowerment, transparency, and strategic development. But it is also a journey that must find a balance between rigour and relevance, one that suits the unique profile of each social enterprise. In Part 2, we'll delve deeper into some of the pitfalls and challenges faced by social enterprises in their quest to measure and maximise their social impact.

Scaling Solutions to Wicked Problems

In the world of social entrepreneurship, the promise of scaling solutions to pressing social problems is a vision that transcends local efforts and seeks to unleash the full potential of innovative initiatives. This vision was/is underpinned by the belief that, by borrowing strategies from the world of business, we can bring these solutions to a global stage.

There was a valid criticism that many of the positive efforts to address social issues remained local and failed to scale; the idea was that by importing business practices, we would be able to scale those efforts, because we know how to grow businesses. Furthermore, the scale of the social issues that we face – the climate and biodiversity crises stand out – make scaling our responses imperative.

Following from this hope and need, there is no shortage of advice on how to scale social enterprises. Different approaches to scaling include:

- Branching: Setting up branches in various countries; legal subsidies that are more or less tightly controlled by the headquarters.
- Affiliation or Social Franchising: Partnering with legal entities not owned by the original organisation but tied to it through a formalised contract (e.g. Tracey & Jarvis, 2007).
- Dissemination: The diffusion of information about the model to recipient organisations in the focal countries can be active, as in providing consulting services, or passive, as in inviting organisations from focal areas/ countries to observe the model in situ.
- Zig-Zagging to Scale: taking side steps in mission-focused activity that can then lead to growth (Rangan & Gregg, 2019).
- El Ebrashi identifies four categories of intangible resources that help social enterprises grow and scale: Human resources, inter-functional coordination, organisational knowledge, and external networks (2018). This study included a range of social enterprise types in Egypt, from NGOs to cooperatives, to unpack how resources shape growth.

In a world where innovation and social/environmental impact are intertwined, the practice of and research on social enterprise scaling offer a treasure trove of possibilities. As the realm of social entrepreneurship continues to evolve, these scaling approaches provide options and ideas for extending the reach and influence of those who seek to make the world a better place. It's not just a promise; it's a call to action. The future belongs to those who dare to scale their social enterprises, for the greater good.

However, when we look at social enterprises and all the great work they are doing, there is a lot less scaling than planned and hoped. We thought that all these amazing business practices would revolutionise social purpose organising. But as is often the case, the reality did not match the expectation. In Part 2, we analyse more closely what happened.

Nurturing Social Enterprise Ecosystems

The ability of social enterprises to grow their social impact isn't solely determined by their own strengths but also by the level of support they receive.

The ecosystem is crucial for a social enterprise. So much so that the ability of those involved in social entrepreneurship as ecosystem builders is core to their very existence (Grassl, 2012).

Box 3.7   Maria Baryamujura, COBATI

The first breakthrough I got was when I participated in the First World Bank Development Marketplace Innovation Competition 2000, and I was among the finalists. I was invited to Washington to do a presentation. For me, though I did not win the money prize, it was a gamechanger. I got to see that my idea was well accepted. I met people from North and South America, from Europe, who are all presenting their ideas. And I was able to share ideas. I was able to learn from them. I was able to get contacts, and when I went back, I was a different person. No one was going to belittle my idea or tell me it was not going to work because the World Bank Development Marketplace gave people like me whose voices were usually ignored an opportunity to put forward our ideas and compete for funding at the World Bank level!

Gonzalez and Dentchev (2021), in their literature review of 258 research papers talking about ecosystems in social entrepreneurship, define three types of support that social enterprises might get from the ecosystem, all of which are critical and feed from each other:

Fuel: This first category deals with the main challenge social enterprises face: Securing resources, funding, skilled personnel, and support. For social enterprises to get this much-needed "fuel" from the ecosystem, certain things are essential:

- **Availability of Resources:** This encompasses financial aid, including grants, donations, and investments, as well as non-financial resources like knowledge, networking, and access to infrastructure.
- **Human Capital:** The effectiveness of social enterprises hinges on the skills and dedication of their staff. Ecosystem actors, including volunteers and organisations, offer hands-on assistance for various tasks.
- **Variety of Actors:** A diverse array of actors, from financial institutions to research organisations and volunteers, play a role in meeting social enterprises' needs. In a well-functioning ecosystem, these actors collaborate and specialise in their roles, enhancing the availability of support.

Hardware: This practical support includes tangible tools, spaces, and specialised services that facilitate social enterprises' growth and positive impact. It involves:

- **Infrastructure:** This encompasses essential elements such as legal advice, accounting assistance, and technical support, which are crucial for the success of social enterprises. Incubators and accelerators also contribute by providing office space, guidance, connections, and professional services.
- **Research and Development:** Universities are key players in ecosystems, granting social enterprises access to advanced technologies, innovations, and knowledge. Other organisations, like corporations, public institutions, and international groups, also work on new knowledge and technologies beneficial to social enterprises.

DNA: Gonzalez and Dentchev (2021) emphasise the significance of the "DNA" of social entrepreneurial ecosystems, which includes cultural and policy aspects impacting social enterprises. This entails:

- **Entrepreneurial Culture:** Creating a culture that encourages and celebrates entrepreneurship is a collective effort involving various actors like government institutions, authorities, incubators, and coworking spaces. They promote entrepreneurship and connect social enterprises with a broader network of supporters, with the government also playing a role by providing grants, organising events, and fostering networking opportunities.
- **Policies:** Governments play a significant role by crafting policies and legal frameworks that simplify the operation of social enterprises. These policies may include grants, streamlined legal requirements (like taxes and reporting), and the use of public resources to support social enterprises.
- **Visibility:** Social enterprises require recognition and visibility for their work. Institutions and interactions within the ecosystem influence how social enterprises are perceived. Achieving recognition can be challenging, as the concept of social enterprises sometimes overlaps with similar notions like social economy and sustainability.

These three types of support are interconnected. For instance, the effectiveness of the "hardware" support depends on the extent of "fuel" support available. In areas with limited resources, accessing specialised services may be challenging due to insufficient demand or suitable conditions. The "DNA" support within an ecosystem enhances this hardware support, promoting infrastructure development and facilitating access to services from universities and other organisations.

The collaboration of various ecosystem actors creates fertile ground for social entrepreneurship to thrive. However, just as social entrepreneurship comes in diverse forms, not all ecosystems are created equal. In the following chapters, we'll delve into the intricate details, exploring how social enterprises navigate these unique challenges, from missing puzzle pieces to disconnected elements.

Box 3.8   Rodrigo Baggio, Recode

When I started the Center for Digital Inclusion in 1995, I started as an entrepreneur solving the need for the democratisation of computers and the Internet. Creating the concept of digital empowerment, the idea itself was very new. Back then, in Brazil, there was no internet outside of university. Proving the concept was difficult. The idea that low-income people could use technologies to get themselves out of poverty was something new. I didn't think of myself as a social entrepreneur at that time. Only when I became an Ashoka Fellow did I realise what it is to be a social entrepreneur, and having this awareness made me a social entrepreneur.

Conclusion

Chapter 3 laid out the four specific areas where social enterprise has shown great promise: Social entrepreneurs, impact, scaling, and ecosystems, backed by research and experience. As discussed, social entrepreneurs embody innovative problem-solving, collaborative leadership, empathy-driven altruism, resilience, risk-taking, visionary leadership, and a commitment to positive social and environmental impact. Measuring this impact offers transformative benefits, including enhanced legitimacy and strategic planning, which will help the social venture scale. But scaling is not evident, as underscored by the complexity of translating successful local efforts into broader impact. Finally, we acknowledge the pivotal role of ecosystems, highlighting the importance of fostering a conducive environment for impactful social entrepreneurship. Part 2 will show how each of these four content areas and the high expectations around them have led to some challenging pitfalls.

References

Aileen Boluk, K., & Mottiar, Z. (2014). Motivations of social entrepreneurs: Blurring the social contribution and profits dichotomy. *Social Enterprise Journal, 10*(1), 53–68.

Bornstein, D. (2004). *How to change the world: Social entrepreneurs and the power of new ideas*. Oxford University Press.

Bowen, H. R. (1953). *Social responsibilities of the businessman*. Harper.

Costa, E., & Andreaus, M. (2021). Social impact and performance measurement systems in an Italian social enterprise: A participatory action research project. *Journal of Public Budgeting, Accounting & Financial Management*, *33*(3), 289–313.

Dey, P., & Steyaert, C. (2016). Rethinking the space of ethics in social entrepreneurship: Power, subjectivity, and practices of freedom. *Journal of Business Ethics*, *133*(4), 627–641.

Di Domenico, M. L., Haugh, H., & Tracey, P. (2010). Social bricolage: Theorizing social value creation in social enterprise. *Entrepreneurship Theory and Practice*, *34*(4), 681–703.

Dufour, B. (2015). *State of the art in social impact measurement: Methods for work integration social enterprises measuring their impact in a public context*. 5th EMES International Research Conference on Social Enterprise: Building a Scientific Field to Foster the Social Enterprise Eco-System. https://hal.archives-ouvertes.fr/hal-01458730/document

El Brashi, R. (2018). Typology of growth strategies and the role of social ventures' intangible resources. *Journal of Small Business and Enterprise Development*, *25*(5), 818–848.

Estrin, S., Mickiewicz, T., & Stephan, U. (2013). Entrepreneurship, social capital, and institutions: Social and commercial entrepreneurship across nations. *Entrepreneurship Theory and Practice*, *37*(3), 479–504.

Glaveli, N., & Geormas, K. (2018). Doing well and doing good: Exploring how strategic and market orientation impacts social enterprise performance. *International Journal of Entrepreneurial Behavior & Research*, *24*(1), 147–170.

Gonzalez, A. D., & Dentchev, N. A. (2021). Ecosystems in support of social entrepreneurs: A literature review. *Social Enterprise Journal*, *17*(3), 329–360.

Grassl, W. (2012). Business models of social enterprise: A design approach to hybridity. *ACRN Journal of Entrepreneurship Perspectives*, *1*(1), 37–60.

Gray, R. (2000). Current developments and trends in social and environmental auditing, reporting, and attestation: A review and comment. *International Journal of Auditing*, *4*(3), 247–268.

Haski-Leventhal, D., & Mehra, A. (2016). Impact measurement in social enterprises: Australia and India. *Social Enterprise Journal*, *12*(1), 78–103.

Kah, S., & Akenroye, T. (2020). Evaluation of social impact measurement tools and techniques: A systematic review of the literature. *Social Enterprise Journal*, *16*(4), 381–402.

Koe Hwee Nga, K., & Shamuganathan, G. (2010). The influence of personality traits and demographic factors on social entrepreneurship start up intentions. *Journal of Business Ethics*, *95*, 259–282.

Lall, S. A. (2019). From legitimacy to learning: How impact measurement perceptions and practices evolve in social enterprise – social finance organization relationships. *VOLUNTAS: International Journal of Voluntary and Nonprofit Organizations*, *30*(3), 562–577.

Luke, B., Barraket, J., & Eversole, R. (2013). Measurement as legitimacy versus legitimacy of measures: Performance evaluation of social enterprise. *Qualitative Research in Accounting & Management, 10*(3–4), 234–258.

Mair, J., & Marti, I. (2006). Social entrepreneurship research: A source of explanation, prediction, and delight. *Journal of World Business, 41*(1), 36–44.

Makhlouf, H. H. (2011). Social entrepreneurship: Generating solutions to global challenges. *International Journal of Management and Information Systems, 15*(1), 1–8.

Martin, L. R., & Osberg, S. (2007). Social entrepreneurship: The case for definition. *Stanford Social Innovation Review, 5*(2), 28–39.

McLoughlin, J., Kaminski, J., Sodagar, B., Khan, S., Harris, R., Arnaudo, G., & McBrearty, S. (2009). A strategic approach to social impact measurement of social enterprises: The SIMPLE methodology. *Social Enterprise Journal, 5*(2), 154–178.

Pangriya, R. (2019). Hidden aspects of social entrepreneurs' life: A content analysis. *Journal of Global Entrepreneurship Research, 9*, 1–19.

Raith, M. G., & Starke, C. (2017). Negotiating the organizational effectiveness of social ventures among multiple stakeholders. *VOLUNTAS: International Journal of Voluntary and Nonprofit Organizations, 28*(4), 1473–1499.

Rangan, K. V., & Gregg, T. (2019). How social entrepreneurs zig-zag their way to impact as scale. *California Management Review, 62*(1), 53–76.

Rawhouser, H., Cummings, M., & Newbert, S. L. (2019). Social impact measurement: Current approaches and future directions for social entrepreneurship research. *Entrepreneurship Theory and Practice, 43*(1), 82–115.

Ruebottom, T. (2011). Counting social change: Outcome measures for social enterprise. *Social Enterprise Journal, 7*(2), 173–182.

Santos, F. M. (2012). A positive theory of social entrepreneurship. *Journal of Business Ethics, 111*(3), 335–351.

Shaw, E., & Carter, S. (2007). Social entrepreneurship: Theoretical antecedents and empirical analysis of entrepreneurial processes and outcomes. *Journal of Small Business and Enterprise Development, 14*, 418–434.

Smith, R., Bell, R., & Watts, H. (2014). Personality trait differences between traditional and social entrepreneurs. *Social Enterprise Journal, 10*(3), 200–221.

Tracey, P., & Jarvis, O. (2007). Toward a theory of social venture franchising. *Entrepreneurship Theory and Practice, 31*(5), 667–685.

Vasakarla, V. (2008). A study on social entrepreneurship and the characteristics of social entrepreneurs. *ICFAI Journal of Management Research, 7*, 32–40.

Part 2
The Pitfalls

4 Social Entrepreneurship beyond Heroism

Managing Self and Others under Emotional Stress

Often, the world of social entrepreneurship is portrayed as a blockbuster movie in which social entrepreneurs are modern-day heroes who swoop in to save the day. Those involved in social entrepreneurship confront some of the world's most wicked problems in resource-scarce environments with limited support. It doesn't take much thought to realise that even trying to solve these problems under such constraints is commendable. Their commitment is admirable, and being surrounded by such admirable people is part of what makes social entrepreneurship an attractive space. Their amazing stories. The innovative solutions they conceptualise. The world needs more like them. And suddenly, they are our heroes. Isn't it great? Or is it? Well, there's more to this story than meets the eye.

Much More than Just a Field of Heroes

There are powerful reasons why social enterprise leaders are personally highlighted and portrayed as aspirational examples. On the one hand, society, especially the young, needs inspirational role models to look up to. On the other hand, the world needs more people willing to bear responsibility for finding solutions to the social and environmental problems we confront. The math is easy to work: You would be hard-pressed to find a better source of inspiration to become the kind of person that the world needs than social entrepreneurs. They are an inspiration for others, and giving them visibility as role models is an impactful endeavour.

Box 4.1   Killian Stokes, Moyee Coffee

I love listening to entrepreneurs tell their stories and how they built their companies. I do think they are heroes. In the business world, we celebrate successful people who've built companies. So why shouldn't we celebrate people who are successful at delivering impact for society? Those people should be celebrated for their work for the community.

DOI: 10.4324/9781003409694-7

And there are also powerful reasons for many social entrepreneurs to jump into the spotlight if offered one. Getting visibility generally aligns with their impact goals. As a social entrepreneur, visibility helps you raise awareness about the issues you care about. Being more visible increases your legitimacy, and this, in turn, makes it less difficult to gather the resources you need to continue to grow your impact. Who wouldn't want to get visibility as a social entrepreneur when getting it checks so many boxes?

In itself, this approach that focuses on the personality of the one heroic leader is not unreasonable. But if we don't balance it with a broader and more humane and empathic look at the people involved in social entrepreneurship, we will have an incomplete picture. Already in 2006, Light, in his influential article *Reshaping Social Entrepreneurship* called our attention to this issue:

> Social entrepreneurship has come to be synonymous with the individual visionary – the risk taker who goes against the tide to start a new organisation to create dramatic social change. The problem with focusing so much attention on the individual entrepreneur is that it neglects to recognise and support thousands of other individuals, groups, and organisations that are crafting solutions to troubles around the globe.
>
> (Light, 2006, p. 47)

Box 4.2   David Nyaluke, Proudly Made in Africa

Being a hero is useful to attract attention to an issue, but in the longer term it is more important to bring along with you the largest number of people that you can, as that will make a bigger difference. The African social entrepreneurs who we work with are treading on a path that very few people have trodden. They are trying very hard to change the way African products reach Europe. . . . They need to bring together a community of interest; the challenges are big, enormous. To succeed you need to work with other people. It may not be an advantage to stand alone as a hero in that sense. . . . Heroism is short-term and maybe helps at the beginning, but long-term you need to work with others and give them importance too. To widen and sustain the impact, you need to bring other people.

We All Are Only Human

Earlier in the book, we explored the qualities and skills that social entrepreneurs tend to show. Among them, a strong prosocial motivation is the core of being a social entrepreneur, whether in nonprofit or for-profit spaces.

Prosocial motivation is simply an academically glamorous way to talk about how strongly social entrepreneurs feel about solving the problems they set themselves to fight. The immense value that social entrepreneurs bring about derives precisely from their prosocial drive, which colours not only their commitment to solving social issues but also how they engage with others in pursuing their goals. Put otherwise, in the case of social entrepreneurs, there is a stronger concern for others in decision-making than in the case of other entrepreneurs (Dong et al., 2022), and this sometimes backfires.

Unfortunately, the excitement about the amazing benefits of social entrepreneurship for society that has overtaken both researchers and social entrepreneurship support ecosystems has limited the attention paid to the darker side of it for those involved (Stephan, 2018). As we have all experienced in many aspects of our lives, professional and personal, avoiding difficult conversations doesn't usually serve anyone well. So let's go for it.

Box 4.3   Catalina Escobar, Fundación Juanfe

Social entrepreneurship is a lonely path. Sometimes you think, is nobody seeing this disaster? They killed a girl from Juanfe in January. And everyone knew it was horrible, but I needed to do something. I knew that we were the voice of the girl. We protested, we made it a media issue, and they put the assassin who killed her in jail. She is the first formally recognised victim of femicide in Cartagena. But her death was going to go unnoticed. How can we allow that? This is not right, and it's frustrating.

Something that social entrepreneurs more often discuss over beers privately than publicly at conferences or in articles is their well-being. Indeed, they often feel rather lonely and overwhelmed by their preoccupations. This happens even when they are surrounded by others who work hand in hand with them. They can experience the responsibility as something so personal that they struggle to share it in ways that might lift some of the weight from their shoulders. When they realise that they are emotionally drained, they struggle to pause or ask for help, used as they are to be the ones supporting others. We make them heroes, but they are only human. They are very admirable humans, like so many people who devote their lives to building a better world. But humans at the end of the day.

There is limited research on the well-being of social entrepreneurs, but that which exists paints a mixed picture. On the one hand, prosocial entrepreneurs who believe they're making a positive impact on society feel happier with their jobs, are less likely to feel burnt out, and are more engaged at work (Brieger et al., 2021). On the other, there is also research showing that having a prosocial motivation as a founder correlates with increased work anxiety (Grant, 2008; Dong et al., 2022; Bolino &Turnley, 2005).

Why are results different across studies? What happens is that much of the research showing improved job satisfaction in prosocial jobs analyses frontline positions (Dong et al., 2022). In the initial stages of launching a social enterprise, as a founder, you do all the frontline work; you get to look in the eye of those whom you are trying to support or engage directly with the natural environment you are contributing to preserving. However, once the organisation begins to grow, the daily tasks of founders and managers of social enterprises often look more like those of any manager than those of a frontline professional.

This stress eases off when you have more control over your work (Kibler et al., 2019), but when the organisations grow, not only does your job as a leader/manager take a different shape, but the freedom you have to choose your role seems to get smaller, not bigger. Fundraising, interviewing for hiring, negotiating contracts, and so forth – these are situations in which the other people involved (funders, candidates, or partners) expect the founder. The limited time some social entrepreneurs end up spending in the field caps the emotional upside, while their freedom to choose the tasks they get involved in feels more restricted. In contrast, they bear a greater sense of responsibility in the face of more difficulties than the ones traditional entrepreneurs face and a greater personal commitment.

Box 4.4   Rodrigo Baggio, Recode

Six or seven years ago, a well-known social entrepreneur from the Middle East committed suicide, and that impacted me a lot. It showed the challenges of being a social entrepreneur. Ashoka did research asking about the biggest challenges of social entrepreneurs, and most talked about loneliness, isolation, and solitude. Skoll awardees also mentioned their well-being at one of the conventions as something important. We need to think about our well-being not as taboo but as something important that we must tackle.

In conclusion, if you are involved in social entrepreneurship, be mindful that you must proactively commit to your own well-being too. Otherwise, your commitment to the well-being of others can quickly become your psychological meat grinder. If you go down (which could happen, trust us on this one), your project might go down with you, which won't do anyone any good.

You are only human, like we all are. We will talk about strategies that seasoned social entrepreneurs use to manage this when we talk about the potential of social entrepreneurship going forward.

Organising Teams for Social Change: A Kind Heart Won't be Enough

Many more people are involved in social entrepreneurship than the founders of social enterprises. Social entrepreneurship at scale, even when there is a main orchestrator (or several), requires a full community of finely tuned performers. There is much research and many books published about team management. If you are scaling a social venture, it might be a good idea to get your hands on a few of them. Here, we are only going to focus on that which is specific to teams in social entrepreneurship. And, guess what? Not all of it is good news.

Box 4.5   Maria Baryamujura, COBATI

You have a strong commitment and get emotionally attached to them. The community people become like family. In the communities, I'm invited to the weddings, funerals, . . . they look upon you. But they also complain. Maria, how come the visitors are not coming? With COVID everything changed. When you are not in touch with them constantly, they go back to what they used to know. My organisation needs the capacity and resources to continue our training programmes among our community partners and to source markets for their products.

As mentioned before, studies show that jobs where you're making a positive impact, like being a hands-on social worker, tend to make people happier and more effective at work. However, this strong motivation to help can backfire in various ways.

Employees involved in projects with a positive social impact often really want to believe they are doing the right thing and that the project will be impactful. This makes them more inclined to stick with even failing strategies (Schaumberg & Wiltermuth, 2014). The stronger the commitment of employees to the initiatives in which they work can make them less critical of their work and that of the organisation and, thus, less prone to identifying potential mistakes and fixing them.

A prosocial motivation can also become a real problem when it pushes employees to take on too much work, making them feel exhausted and burnt out (Bolino & Grant, 2016; Grant, 2008; Grant & Sumanth, 2009). In other words, just because someone works for a social cause, that won't make them necessarily happy. Stress can take away the joy of it quickly (Bolino et al., 2015; Kibler et al., 2019). This happens for both entrepreneurs and employees. However, the way this works out is different for each group. For entrepreneurs, the not-so-happy effect of wanting to help goes away when they have more control over their work (which, as we already discussed, is not always the case). But for employees, this effect changes based on whether they really enjoy their work or not. They can manage more stress while still being happy if they have a strong intrinsic motivation.

Another negative element that sometimes kicks in for employees working in social enterprises is citizenship fatigue. This basically means that they get tired of trying to help others. They eventually feel like they've done their fair share of good deeds already and decide to move on to a more me-centred lifestyle they've now earned the right to. This tends to occur when they feel like their organisations aren't giving them the support they require. However, chances of citizenship fatigue decrease if they have strong, positive bonds with teammates (Bolino et al., 2015).

Along the same lines, employees who are in very close connection to the suffering of beneficiaries might experience what is called "compassion fatigue," which takes a toll in the form of sadness, anxiety, bad attitudes towards work, and, ultimately, reduced effectiveness (Adams et al., 2006; Figley, 1995). This fatigue is more profound. It doesn't derive from working too much but from experiencing the suffering of those you are trying to help very closely while feeling unable to help as much as you'd wish to (Klimecki & Singer, 2012).

Box 4.6   Killian Stokes, Moyee Coffee

There are strong personalities; you need strong characters to build an organisation. And you'll have employees that go, yeah, well, Darryl is a bit of a jerk to work with, things like that. Whether you run a company or a social enterprise, you should have a culture, be mindful of your bellicose ways, and be careful how you treat people. Sometimes we do need that to bring about change, the people who can be controversial.

Finally, prosocial supervisors might be overly lenient when evaluating employee performance. This limits transparency, damaging the ability of the organisation to assess employees' contributions fairly. Consequently, it stalls employee growth and might even result in people being promoted to their levels of incompetence (Peter & Hull, 1969), leaving more deserving candidates behind (Bolino et al., 2015). If you're leading or managing a social enterprise, you've got it wrong if you think your team's passion for solving the problems you focus on will automatically translate into happiness, engagement, and high performance. Indeed, for employees in social enterprises, this increased happiness might not always be there, nor will the team's performance always be optimal. You will need to develop specific strategies to avoid these pitfalls.

Making Decisions about Scaling, Downscaling, Success, and Failure

In this book, we are devoting Chapters 6 and 10 to the scaling of social enterprises. In this chapter, we will just briefly mention how the pressure and focus on the personality of the founders/managers can affect their capacity to manage their organisations effectively. For social entrepreneurship to live up to its promise, we need successful social entrepreneurs who can focus their energy and resources effectively and scale their impact over time. However, the extra pressure social entrepreneurs endure is obviously damaging for them, and it also causes some of them to quit their projects to protect their health (Dong et al., 2022).

On the other extreme, this pressure makes it terribly difficult for some social entrepreneurs to let go of their projects. Even when they suspect that doing something different with their time, energy, and commitment would be more conducive to solving the issues they care about, they can't get to terms with the idea of moving on. Just the thought of it seems somewhat wrong, somewhat unethical. But deploying resources effectively in the fight for a cause is as much about knowing where to use them as it is about knowing where not to. It is important to know when to stop. We need social entrepreneurs to live to fight another day. We need to break the taboo on moving on from a social enterprise, be it because someone else takes the role or be it because you close the operation to do something else.

Not surprisingly, given all the above, there is a controversial relationship between the prosocial motivation of social entrepreneurs and the exit strategy (Dong et al., 2022). Disengaging from the project you founded is always emotionally difficult, especially if it means closing the organisation. But in the case of social enterprises, it is especially devastating (Mcmullen & Bergman, 2017). And, due to the burden of gender roles, it is more acute in the case of women, who seem to find it even harder to end their engagement in social enterprises (Dickel & Eckardt, 2021). The positive reading is that social entrepreneurs, especially women, are more committed. As a funder (donor or impact investor), you can rest assured that they will go down with the organisation if need be. The negative reading is that they might be pushing it beyond the point at which they deplete resources in projects that are not so impactful and burn themselves along the way, reducing their chances of launching other potentially more impactful endeavours.

But this strife doesn't only happen in the more extreme case of having to close the organisation. When the time comes to restructure, as is often necessary when any organisation evolves, social entrepreneurs find it difficult to make necessary management decisions to downscale or even completely cancel parts of their operations. This usually involves firing people or even letting go of initiatives that generate value for beneficiaries. But it is necessary for the organisation's survival or to put resources into a more impactful project.

Box 4.7   João Magalhães, Code For All

I think there's a romantic view that we are very nice guys and very friendly. And I think I'm a good guy. But it's part of my job to sometimes make tough decisions. And it's not easy. During the pandemic we had to close several locations. We were having a lot of impact on some of those locations. But they were not sustainable under COVID. It was really hard. Some people saw us like, these guys, because now things get more difficult, they just close and leave. And that's the kind of difficult decisions that sometimes you need to make. Because if the location is not sustainable you are putting the whole organisation at risk.

The way in which emotions get so much in the way of organisational decision-making to the point of sometimes being damaging is not an unmovable trait of social entrepreneurs. Rather, it is a characteristic that they show specifically when confronted with a decision related to a social venture, but not in other contexts. Munoz and Cacciotti (2014) show that social entrepreneurs react emotionally when their social venture goes through tough times. Up to here, it is what we would have expected. Interestingly, they find that the same person will handle failure more rationally in a traditional business situation. They will analyse the situation, make plans, and strategise without letting emotions get so in the way. There is still a lot to understand about how getting involved in one kind of project or another affects how the person makes decisions. Social entrepreneurs need to be empowered to pull out the right set of tools (emotional and rational), as appropriate, rather than betting it all on some heroic fibre that social entrepreneurs may have.

Social Entrepreneurs Wanted. Heroes Only.
Others Refrain

One of the main goals of giving social entrepreneurs visibility is for their stories to inspire others to create social enterprises that might contribute to solving social and environmental problems. We put them on stage and speak wonders of them, among other reasons, for others to look at them and think:

"I want to be like you" or, even better: "I'm going to be like you." But what kind of person looks at someone who is being portrayed as this perfect, all-powerful hero and feels like they can be like them? If we turn social entrepreneurship into a space for heroes, who will rise to the bar?

People traditionally discriminated against, like women, tend to be more self-critical and self-select out of opportunities. In the previous example, rather than thinking, "I'm going to be like you," some of them would tend to think "I wish I were like you; unfortunately, I'm not." By conveying this heroic image and avoiding talking about the vulnerabilities, are we inducing an unconscious discrimination of who might aspire to be a social entrepreneur? Portraying social entrepreneurs as heroes might not help make social entrepreneurship a truly universal and inclusive reality. We might be pushing away the people who might precisely be more drawn to it given their own experiences of discrimination.

Evidence from successful social entrepreneurs indicates that achieving success is more about skills that can be learned rather than just personal traits. These skills include things like raising awareness, gathering funds, negotiating effectively, and handling the challenging changes that come with growing an organisation from its beginning stages to a well-established state (Light, 2006). If this is the case, many more people can potentially be successful social entrepreneurs, regardless of how heroic they feel.

Conclusion

It's crucial to acknowledge that social entrepreneurs, being human, have limitations, make mistakes, and require self-care. Overemphasising individual leaders risks neglecting the significant contributions of communities and teams, along with the unique challenges they face. Moreover, portraying social entrepreneurs as rare heroes may discourage many from considering engagement in social entrepreneurship. Our love of social entrepreneurs is rightful and driven by good intentions and solid reasons. However, if not managed properly by them and by the organisations in their ecosystems, it can be very damaging for social entrepreneurs and for social entrepreneurship as a whole. We might need to save social entrepreneurship from our uncontrolled love of it.

References

Adams, R. E., Boscarino, J. A., & Figley, C. R. (2006). Compassion fatigue and psychological distress among social workers: A validation study. *American Journal of Orthopsychiatry*, *76*, 103–108.

Bolino, M. C., & Grant, A. M. (2016). The bright side of being prosocial at work, and the dark side, too: A review and agenda for research on other-oriented motives, behavior, and impact in organizations. *Academy of Management Annals*, *10*(1), 599–670.

Bolino, M. C., Hsiung, H. H., Harvey, J., & LePine, J. A. (2015). "Well, I'm tired of tryin'!" Organizational citizenship behavior and citizenship fatigue. *Journal of Applied Psychology, 100*(1), 56.

Bolino, M. C., & Turnley, W. H. (2005). The personal costs of citizenship behavior: The relationship between individual initiative and role overload, job stress, and work-family conflict. *Journal of Applied Psychology, 90*(4), 740.

Brieger, S. A., De Clercq, D., & Meynhardt, T. (2021). Doing good, feeling good? Entrepreneurs' social value creation beliefs and work-related wellbeing. *Journal of Business Ethics, 172,* 707–725.

Dickel, P., & Eckardt, G. (2021). Who wants to be a social entrepreneur? The role of gender and sustainability orientation. *Journal of Small Business Management, 59*(1), 196–218.

Dong, J., Wang, X., Cao, X., & Higgins, D. (2022). More prosocial, more ephemeral? The role of work-related wellbeing and gender in incubating social entrepreneurs' exit intention. *International Journal of Environmental Research and Public Health, 19*(7), 3999. https://doi.org/10.3390/ijerph19073999

Figley, C. R. (1995). Compassion fatigue as secondary traumatic stress disorder: An overview. In C. R. Figley (Ed.), *Compassion fatigue* (pp. 1–20). Brunner/Mazel.

Grant, A. M. (2008). Does intrinsic motivation fuel the prosocial fire? Motivational synergy in predicting persistence, performance, and productivity. *Journal of Applied Psychology, 93*(1), 48.

Grant, A. M., & Sumanth, J. J. (2009). Mission possible? The performance of prosocially motivated employees depends on manager trustworthiness. *Journal of Applied Psychology, 94*(4), 927.

Kibler, E., Wincent, J., Kautonen, T., Cacciotti, G., & Obschonka, M. (2019). Can prosocial motivation harm entrepreneurs' subjective well-being? *Journal of Business Venturing, 34*(4), 608–624.

Klimecki, O., & Singer, T. (2012). Empathic distress fatigue rather than compassion fatigue? Integrating findings from empathy research in psychology and social neuroscience. *Pathological Altruism, 5,* 368–383.

Light, P. C. (2006). Reshaping social entrepreneurship. *Stanford Social Innovation Review, 4*(3), 47–51.

McMullen, J. S., & Bergman Jr, B. J. (2017). Social entrepreneurship and the development paradox of prosocial motivation: A cautionary tale. *Strategic Entrepreneurship Journal, 11*(3), 243–270.

Munoz, P., & Cacciotti, G. (2014, June 4–7). *Understanding failure and exit in social entrepreneurship: A protocol analysis of coping strategies.* Proceedings of the Babson College Entrepreneurship Research Conference, London.

Peter, L. J., & Hull, R. (1969). *The peter principle* (Vol. 4). London: Souvenir Press.

Schaumberg, R. L., & Wiltermuth, S. S. (2014). Desire for a positive moral self-regard exacerbates escalation of commitment to initiatives with prosocial aims. *Organizational Behavior and Human Decision Processes, 123*(2), 110–123.

Stephan, U. (2018). Entrepreneurs' mental health and well-being: A review and research agenda. *Academy of Management Perspectives, 32*(3), 290–322.

5 Impact – the Trend, the Pressure, and the Reality of Social Change

Measuring impact is a popular trend. Everyone is supposed to be measuring their impact these days, from researchers, to educators, to doctors, to social entrepreneurs. In nonprofit studies, this is called the "outcomes movement" (Brest, 2020), which is the increased attention over the past two decades to measuring and reporting social impact, beyond *what* you do, to the *difference* that you have made in the world. As we saw in Chapter 3, measuring impact has evolved from two traditions, business and philanthropy/nonprofit, and it has enabled social entrepreneurs to demonstrate and even monetise the value they create. Our focus here is on the pitfalls of social impact measurement, based on research, literature, and our work with practitioners trying to deliver, measure, and report social impact.

Because it is so much easier to understand, describe, and measure activities and outputs, those are often reported as impact. Go to the website of your favourite social enterprise. You should find some statement about their impact. This might sound like: We have trained 500 fishermen on environmentally friendly coastal economic activities or served 100 hot breakfasts to disadvantaged children. This is all fabulous. But it is not impact. It is *what* you have done, not the change you have brought about.

Depending on the size and available resources of the social enterprise, it may not be possible or desirable for the organisation to measure its own longer-term impact, but rather a funder may be better placed to do so (Ebrahim & Rangan, 2014). However, in private at least, social entrepreneurs, changemakers, and nonprofit managers often express frustration with funder-driven impact measurement. This frustration is because funders often focus on a shorter timeframe, like the duration of a grant, and are primarily interested in only the part of the social enterprise they are supporting. Moreover, funders often expect social enterprises to measure the impact themselves. When several funders are looking for impact reports, this can become a tedious exercise for managers, and the bigger picture of understanding mission progress can get lost. In particular, grant reporting can be very detailed and time-consuming.

DOI: 10.4324/9781003409694-8

Some grant-givers refer to their funds as "investments" looking for a social return on that investment. This is not only a time-consuming process for the grant recipient, but it is often a bit of theatre, trying to make what often continues to be traditional grant-giving sound more commercial. Part of the reason we report outcomes as impact is because it is so hard to measure impact. It is more straightforward to measure activities, like training 500 people, or outcomes, like diverting 10 tonnes of food from landfill as a result of your activities.

In order to delve a bit deeper into the challenges of impact for social entrepreneurs, we provide an example of social impact. A common way to understand impact is through a Logical Model Framework, also called a "social impact value chain" or Theory of Change, that is essentially a table that helps you align your vision and mission, with your activities, resources, outcomes, outputs, and impact.

Shuttle Knit is a Company Limited by Guarantee and social enterprise based in Wicklow Town, Ireland. It was founded in 2001 by a small group of women within the Wicklow Traveller Group who were working to empower Traveller women in their community through employment and training. Travellers are Ireland's indigenous nomadic people who have been discriminated against for generations. Policies to address Traveller issues were usually attempts to turn them into settled people, seeing them as a scourge on society, rather than a distinct ethnic group. Statistics show a stark difference in social outcomes for Travellers in comparison with settled people, such as life expectancy (65 years), third level education attainment, suicide rates, rates of unemployment, and so forth (Tobin et al., 2020) with 80% of Traveller women unemployed (Government of Ireland, 2021). Shuttle Knit founders were motivated to address these poor social outcomes and discrepancies by providing employment for Traveller women in an area of work, knitting and sales, where they traditionally had skills and knowledge.

The founders obtained a small grant to create a knitting group, which evolved into a formal organisation that employed Traveller women to design, create, and sell handcrafted knitwear. The mission of the organisation is: "To improve quality of life for Traveller Women and their families through enterprise and to combat negative attitudes towards Travellers, by demonstrating their skills through the Shuttle Knit products" (www.shuttleknit.com). It is clear from the Logical Model Framework in Table 5.1 the difference between outcomes, that are within the organisation and more easily measurable, and longer-term impact, such as changing public attitudes, that are much harder to measure and take place in wider society outside the boundaries of the organisation.

Table 5.1 Shuttle Knit Logical Model Framework

Activities	Resources	Outputs	Outcomes	Impact
Inside the organisation			**Outside the organisation**	
Employ 11 Traveller women.	Salaries are part funded by Irish Government and part funded by generated sales revenue.	Increased confidence and well-being among staff.	Wicklow Traveller community has role models of successful working women.	Increased employment among Traveller women in Ireland.
Design and create handcrafted knitwear.	Production staff, board members, managers.	Beautiful original handcrafted knitwear.	Increased skills of staff.	More employable Travellers.
Sell knitwear via four channels: Markets, online, wholesale, walk-ins.	Sales manager, board member with relevant sales expertise, grants for web development.	Communications materials, stories of Travellers' experiences, social media posts, short videos on creative outputs.	Increased skills, consumers in Ireland and abroad wearing Shuttle Knit products.	More positive public attitude towards Travellers, less discrimination in education and employment.

Box 5.1   João Magalhães, Code For All

We measure a lot of impact indicators. We attain 98% of employment for our students, many of whom were unemployed or underemployed. But this is not the only impact. We also impact their families or the companies where they work. We also have impact on the national budget because in 4 months we transform the cost of an unemployed person into an income through tax. So the social return on investment is huge.

As well as our adult programme, we have another solution to introduce computer science in the education systems. In that case it is difficult to measure impact because it's a medium-term, long-term view, and not like something that you can measure in 3 months or 4 months. We started tracking improvement on the maths grade. Our students improved the maths grades when compared to students in other schools from 11% to 17%. But this is not our end goal. I believe the huge impact would be when these kids are 19 or 20 years old.

Attribution and Causation

Critical challenges with impact are those of attribution and causation. Attribution is to what extent a social enterprise can attribute a social or environmental change to the organisation's activities. Causation is to what extent a social enterprise can claim to have caused a social change. In reality, the extent to which one person or one organisation can claim social impact as their own is questionable. Social impact is always intricately part of a wider social context that has many influences, actors, and pressures. For example, reduced unemployment rate or less single-use plastic in circulation might be the goal of social enterprises, and they may have done great work towards those goals, but as with all social issues, there is not one simple cause and effect. Unemployment rates are influenced by macro-economic trends, demographic changes, to name a few factors. This applies to the mission of Shuttle Knit above; the unemployment rate of Traveller women in Ireland is influenced by many factors beyond the scope of that one organisation. Single-use plastic is influenced by consumer trends and the growing awareness of the problem of plastic pollution and fossil fuel use, among other issues. So, claims of impact are either reporting activities and outputs (which might be more realistic) or actually overstating their impact (which then hurts their credibility). Neither option is a great look, and they both create tensions for social entrepreneurs that they could really do without. As a result, a pitfall of impact measurement is that it tends to be reductionist, underestimating the complexity of bringing about positive change.

The outcomes movement pressures social entrepreneurs in two ways: To tell powerful impact stories and implement complex impact measurement tools and strategies. The pressure to tell powerful impact stories can result in overstating the impact, and boosting the hero narrative, as we saw in Chapter 4. When a social entrepreneur stands up and tells the powerful story of their impact, donors and investors are delighted. Crowds are wooed. It makes for a great TED talk. But it puts the social entrepreneur on a pedestal that is far removed from the gritty reality of working towards a social or environmental goal. The second pressure resulting from the emphasis on impact is that the tools and strategies for measuring impact are complex, consuming precious human and financial resources (Moran & Ward-Christie, 2022). For-profit social enterprises sometimes prefer regular venture capital money to impact investment money because of the workload that impact investors impose in terms of impact measurement.

The Impact of Funders and Impact Investors

If a funder wants causation and attribution addressed to decide whether the social enterprise is actually impactful, then we need to consider the counterfactual. The counterfactual is the future that would have existed had you not implemented a given action. So as an impact-oriented organisation, you need to ask yourself to what extent are you generating a future that is better than the future that would have existed had you not implemented this action? The real impact is not about measuring Time 1 versus Time 0. It's about how that difference compares to what would have happened in that same time interval in the absence of your intervention. This data is more accessible in medical research (treatment and control groups), but much harder in other realms when it is difficult or impossible to have or find a control group.

But those funding social enterprises should be thinking also about the attribution and additionality of their own impact (Ebrahim & Rangan, 2014). As a funder, it is just as easy to fall into the "hero" trap as it is for a social entrepreneur. Labelling yourself as an impact investment fund will get you many invitations to conferences where you can participate in endless discussions about why you are so much purer than BlackRock. The problem with most impact investment funds, from an impact perspective, is that they "shop" from a very short list of companies that they tend to shorten even further as soon as they start their due diligence. Few social enterprises in the funnel are at the same time "pure" enough and mature enough to entail a level of risk that the fund is comfortable with. In the end, they all want the same few social enterprises.

Additionality of the impact speaks of how your impact is truly additional to what others are doing. Are you just crowding out other similar solutions that would have had the same impact? With the previous discussion about the counterfactual and additionality in mind, if an impact fund invests only in social enterprises that already have a strong impact and are growing, are they having an impact? Well, their Theory of Change might be that without their investment, the social enterprise wouldn't be able to grow. But is that true in a market where virtually every fund seeks the same venture profile? Not really. They would just be investing in a company that would have been funded anyway by someone else. There is no additionality versus the counterfactual.

Social Impact versus Social Change

Whether you are an investor or entrepreneur or manager, you need to ask yourself what are you trying to do here: Measure impact or bring about positive change? Depending on your social mission, you might need to ease up on the former in order to attain the latter. Many social enterprises have a mission that implicitly or explicitly claims to make change. Social movement studies provide several decades of research on how civil society organises to bring about positive change (e.g. Jasper, 2011). Specific initiatives focus on advocacy, lobbying, political activity, and mobilising people and involve informal groups which often then formalise (Lima, 2021). While researchers have studied social movements separately, in departments of political science, history, and sociology, and in separate academic journals, there are overlaps with social entrepreneurship. In fact, this separation has resulted in a lack of sharing of learning between the different disciplines.

From a sociological perspective, drawing on institutional theory, social change can be understood as a change in legitimacy (Cannon, 2020). Legitimacy is the taken for granted assumption that a certain practice, belief, or action is right, appropriate, and good (Suchman, 1995). Legitimacy is often not noticed – comprising the taken for granted assumptions that shape how we see the world. Another feature of legitimacy is that it is specific to a time and place, yet we tend to see it as fixed. Over the course of history, legitimacy changes, and different cultures and traditions have different legitimacy beliefs. In other words, it is a socially constructed phenomenon. However, people tend to see it and talk about it as an objective truth. An example is the traditional idea that being a "good husband" involved making enough money so that your wife didn't have to work. A woman that didn't work was assumed to be a woman better taken care of. Today, however, many social enterprises have a mission to support women towards employment or to advance their careers. The legitimacy of the practice has changed in the recent past and is seen as absolute and fixed now, as it was then.

Box 5.2   Catalina Escobar, Fundación Juanfe

Last year, of more than 1,200 girls who accessed Juanfe, 54% wanted to commit suicide. By the end of the year, we lowered it to 8%. The model works, but what are these horrible statistics? It is because of their vulnerability, because of the abuses they've suffered. It is not enough that they become the best professionals. They will drop out of work if they have difficulties at home. So we work on the technical and emotional scaffolding of the girls. It takes us 2 years per girl, but they get out of poverty. And their children, grandchildren, great-grandchildren . . . they get out of poverty with them.

The Social Entrepreneur's Legitimacy Paradox

When social entrepreneurs advocate for a social change that goes against the status quo, they are challenging current legitimacy beliefs. We also know from a long line of research that founders need to have legitimacy in order to attract enough resources to start up a new venture (Zimmerman & Zeitz, 2002). So the social entrepreneur simultaneously wants to challenge legitimacy but needs it to start up an organisation that can bring about social change. She needs the thing that she is trying to change. This is the social entrepreneur's legitimacy paradox.

To illustrate this legitimacy paradox, we return to the case of Shuttle Knit. Their experience and market research have shown that consumers are unlikely to purchase products made by Travellers, so the Traveller identity of the knitwear does not feature prominently on the product. If Shuttle Knit promoted the fact that these were products made by Travellers, this would support their mission and vision – to change society's attitude towards Travellers. But promoting or even stating that the product was designed and made by Travellers would simultaneously hinder their ability to sell the product, the main activity of the organisation. This is the legitimacy paradox. Shuttle Knit needs the legitimacy from the system it is trying to change in order to operate as a retail business.

Returning to measuring impact, how do you measure changes in legitimacy?

Measuring Social Change?

Research on social movements provides numerous examples of how measuring individual behaviour serves to analyse social change or changes in legitimacy. For example, sociologists have created artificial online systems to study behaviour and calculate the critical mass needed to trigger a tipping point that will change a social convention (Centola et al., 2018). That research follows a trend in social movement studies that shifted from looking at institutional or high-level systems (grand theories) to understand social change towards more individual-level behavioural or agentic approaches (Jasper, 2010). Social entrepreneurship research is dominated by agentic approaches, perhaps partly because the topic is applied and based at business schools. In this chapter we are concerned with the problems and challenges of measuring impact, and what happens when we try to consider impact, not just as counting activities, but as social change. This shift suggests an increased awareness of levels; while much focus has been on organisational activities, we also need to consider and understand how that relates to macro-level societal change.

Box 5.3   Killian Stokes, Moyee Coffee

The big question that we now realise needs to be asked is: Can revenue generated by a social enterprise bring about social change? That is the big question. And it is a long-term question. When we started, we didn't realise that was the question we were exploring. It has been satisfying. It is a body of work. You have to do many years of plodding along, of almost mundane work, in order to figure out that big question. It has become my career. Does it have an impact? I don't know how much you can quantify the last seven years.

Levels of Social Change

Zahra et al. (2009) provided a typology of social entrepreneurs that helps us distinguish between the levels and extent of social change involved in an initiative. Social bricoleurs work at a local level, drawing on local knowledge to address a specific challenge. Social constructionists work on a larger scale taking advantage of opportunities, or unmet needs, to bring about more significant social change, but still not challenging the legitimacy of the existing system. Social engineers, who are rare, are those who transform systems, challenging the status quo, and catalysing the creation of new systems, or approaches. Social engineers, like Father Arizmendi of Mondragón, or Mohammad Yunus of the Grameen bank, replace legitimacy beliefs. Yunus challenged the assumption that banks should only lend to borrowers who had capital to ensure they could repay a loan. He lent to poor people who did not have any way to show that they could repay the loan. Yet their rate of return was significantly higher than standard banks (Morduch, 1999). Turning the assumptions around risks and loans on their head. But remember the legitimacy paradox? Bankers did not think Yunus was a hero; many thought he was mad (Hackett, 2010), making his task all the more challenging, and his success all the more impressive.

Social entrepreneurs often feel pressure to have macro-level impact, which can be harmful. Social entrepreneurs might aim for macro-level societal change, but their initiatives are often more likely to be incremental local actions (Cannon & Dart, 2022). Such transformative change is referred to in entrepreneurship as the Schumpeterian approach to disrupting markets, and is encouraged through pitching competitions, funding awards, the popularity of the concept of digital disruption, and through the heroization of the social entrepreneurs that we saw in Chapter 4. While the intention is transformative change, the reality involves much more collaboration with existing actors, trial and error attempts, and then smaller contributions than initially envisaged. This more gradual approach to impact is referred to in entrepreneurship literature as the Hayekian approach. The experience of digital social entrepreneurs reflects the pressure to have big impact and bring about big social change. Whereas the reality is often something more moderate.

A final point about the problem of ignoring levels when considering social impact and social change is that we often neglect systemic power inequalities. Social entrepreneurship has been rightly criticised for sometimes making systemic issues into individual challenges and ignoring the serious barriers that systemic inequalities cause for some individuals and not for others. In overlooking power structures and institutional history, social entrepreneurs can put unreasonable pressure on individuals to address the systemic structural power imbalances that negatively affect those same beneficiaries (historic, racial, cultural, social). An example of this are programmes that tell women to "lean in" to address gender inequality in the workplace. Not to say it's all bad; some might find this a positive experience. But, because of ignoring systemic inequalities, they tend to focus only on employment or career development, as if there is a level playing field, and ignore other kinds of necessary interventions. As a feature of social entrepreneurship, ignoring levels of change/impact/mission is a challenge that we need to acknowledge and discuss far more than we have to date.

Conclusion

While the outcomes movement has increased attention paid to social impact, many of the approaches have been reductionist. For many social entrepreneurs, especially those working on a local level delivering missing services, measuring what they achieve, whether it is outcomes or impact, is an important way to illustrate and prove the value of their work. While impact implies some kind of social change, what we know from social movements has eluded social entrepreneurs, who are hanging between two extremes: Being heroes (full of legitimacy) or being social pariahs (when they challenge legitimacy). How can social enterprises move beyond this conundrum? Do they have to choose between an over-simplified approach to impact measurement, or try to tackle the complexities of challenging legitimacy and social change? Largely, this depends on their mission and the type and level of change they are aiming for. In part three we return to impact to explore ways forward to overcome the problems of reductionism, legitimacy challenges, and social change.

References

Brest, P. (2020). The outcomes movement in philanthropy and the non-profit sector. In W. W. Powell & P. Bromley (Eds.), *The nonprofit sector: A research handbook* (Chapter 16, 3rd ed., pp. 381–408). Stanford University Press.

Cannon, S. M. (2020). Legitimacy as property and process: The case of an Irish LGBT organization. *VOLUNTAS: International Journal of Voluntary and Nonprofit Organizations*, *31*, 39–55. https://doi.org/10.1007/s11266-019-00091-x

Cannon, S. M., & Dart, R. (2022). The emergence and evolution of digital social ventures in Dublin, Ireland. *Nonprofit and Voluntary Sector Quarterly*, *52*(6). https://doi.org/10.1177/08997640221139430

Centola, D., Becker, J., Brackbill, D., & Baronchelli, A. (2018). Experimental evidence for tipping points in social convention. *Science*, *360*(6393), 1116–1119. https://doi.org/10.1126/science.aas8827

Ebrahim, A., & Rangan, V. K. (2014). What impact? A framework for measuring the scale and scope of social performance. *California Management Review*, *56*, 118–141. https://doi.org/10.1525/cmr.2014.56.3.118

Government of Ireland. (2021). *Final report of the joint committee on key issues affecting the Traveller community* (33/JCKITC/01, pp. 1–102). Houses of theOireachtas.www.oireachtas.ie/en/committees/33/committee-on-key-issues-affecting-the-traveller-community/

Hackett, M. T. (2010). Challenging social enterprise debates in Bangladesh. *Social Enterprise Journal*, *6*(3), 210–224. ABI/INFORM Global; Social Science Premium Collection. https://doi.org/10.1108/17508611011088814

Jasper, J. M. (2010). Social movement theory today: Toward a theory of action? *Sociology Compass*, *4*(11), 965–976. https://doi.org/10.1111/j.1751-9020.2010.00329.x

Jasper, J. M. (2011). Emotions and social movements: Twenty years of theory and research. *Annual Review of Sociology*, *37*, 285–303. JSTOR.

Lima, V. (2021). The institutionalisation of social movements: Co-optation and democratic policy-making. *Political Studies Review*, *19*(2), 245–261. https://doi.org/10.1177/1478929920913805

Moran, M., & Ward-Christie, L. (2022). Blended social impact investment transactions: Why are they so complex? *Journal of Business Ethics*, *179*(4), 1011–1031. https://doi.org/10.1007/s10551-022-05153-7

Morduch, J. (1999). The role of subsidies in microfinance: Evidence from the Grameen bank. *Journal of Development Economics*, *60*(1), 229–248. https://doi.org/10.1016/S0304-3878(99)00042-5

Suchman, M. C. (1995). Managing legitimacy: Strategic and institutional approaches. *Academy of Management Review*, *20*(3), 571–610.

Tobin, M., Lambert, S., & McCarthy, J. (2020). Grief, tragic death, and multiple loss in the lives of Irish Traveller community health workers. *OMEGA – Journal of Death and Dying*, *81*(1), 130–154. https://doi.org/10.1177/0030222818762969

Zahra, S. A., Gedajlovic, E., Neubaum, D. O., & Shulman, J. M. (2009). A typology of social entrepreneurs: Motives, search processes and ethical challenges. *Special Issue Ethics and Entrepreneurship, 24*(5), 519–532. https://doi.org/10.1016/j.jbusvent.2008.04.007

Zimmerman, M. A., & Zeitz, G. J. (2002). Beyond survival: Achieving new venture growth by building legitimacy. *Academy of Management Review, 27*(3), 414–431. https://doi.org/10.5465/amr.2002.7389921

6 Scaling Wisely

Making Choices That Prioritise Impact

Much has been written about scaling social enterprises. Well, let's cut to the chase on it. Conventional wisdom often aligns organisational growth with success. If someone runs a big organisation, they must be important. If they run a small one, . . . nah! Surely not so important. The impetus behind that focus is the assumption that organisational growth is always good, which of course, originates in the market logic where growing profit is the goal. But when it comes to social enterprises, their primary goal is to impact a specific group of beneficiaries or the planet positively, and the rest is means to ends. Thus, when you think about social entrepreneurship scaling, what do you think they should be scaling? That's right, they should be scaling their impact! You may be left wondering: Is that not the same thing as growing the organisation? We'll get back to this in a second.

In Chapter 5 we discussed impact, the outcomes movement, and the problems with the pressure to tell impact stories. In this chapter, we build on the concept of impact because when we talk about scaling social enterprises, we mean scaling impact. When scaling, it is important for social entrepreneurs to understand, similar to what other enterprises/organisations need to consider: If their idea is ready to scale, and if there is a receptive audience for it, what resources are needed, what the potential risks are, and so forth. But, most importantly, social entrepreneurs must consider how scaling will increase the impact (Dees et al., 2004). So once again, we need to consider levels of social change. Only then can they figure out what strategy and methods to use. So how do social entrepreneurs or social enterprise managers go about this?

There are many books, articles, consultants, and websites that give advice on how to scale social enterprises, and we don't want to simply list those out here. Instead, we provide a framework of three different approaches to scaling according to the level/type of social change they are aiming for, illustrated in Figure 6.1. Based on the literature and our work with social enterprises, we have categorised the approaches into: Scaling up, scaling out, and scaling wide. This framework is practical because it can help you to analyse and understand the strengths and weaknesses of any scaling advice that you come

DOI: 10.4324/9781003409694-9

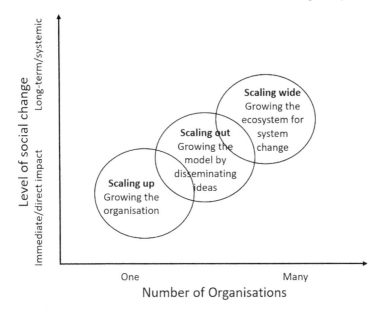

Figure 6.1 Three approaches to scaling impact

across in your reading and practice, and help you decide which approach to scaling is a good fit for your organisation's mission.

The distinctions between the three different approaches to scaling relate to what the social enterprise is trying to scale and how, considering foremost different levels of social change. Many of the scaling methods we have found can fit into one of these three approaches.

- What is usually referred to as simply "scaling," we call the **scaling up** approach. It means growing the organisational structure in order to grow immediate outcomes and impact. This is a good fit with organisations that deliver a socially beneficial product or service and often linked with early stages of a social entrepreneur's journey in trying to bring about social change.
- In **scaling out**, the goal is also to scale impact, but this does not necessarily require scaling organisational size. Partnerships, diffusion of practices, and collaborations (growing the influence) will all grow longer-term impact and advance a social mission without necessarily growing organisational size.

- The **scaling wide** approach aims to scale higher-level social change, which is beyond the impact of any one organisation. Scaling wide involves efforts to grow the ecosystem and to mobilise more actors to achieve high-level social change or system change. System change refers to change in policy, practices, beliefs, legitimacy, and values. Social entrepreneurs often take on longer-term change goals later in their careers, as their social missions mature.

We find this framework of three approaches helpful in order to distinguish between levels of change when matching scaling strategies with social missions. These three approaches reflect pure types of scaling, but in reality scaling strategies might borrow from different approaches, change over time, or create something entirely new. And, surely, each of the three comes with challenges.

Box 6.1   Rodrigo Baggio, Recode

We inspire companies, governments, and foundations to promote digital empowerment themselves. We want it replicated with us or without us. It is one thing to grow your organisation and it is a different thing to grow the impact. You can grow the impact without growing the organisation. There are three levels. Firstly, you can grow the organisation. Secondly, you can work with government to turn your innovation into a public service. Finally, you can work with others, creating a movement, a coalition. You can scale up in a proprietary way or in an open-source way and then the evolution of the social entrepreneur is to think of themselves as an orchestrator operating a collaborative movement to provide systems change, rather than as the leader of their organisation.

Scaling Up: Growing the Organisation

Scaling up is an approach to scaling that focuses on organisational growth and direct impact. It is the approach that is more prevalent in textbooks that rush into "when and how to scale" with the assumption that it is clear what we are scaling and that scaling is the right thing to do. This is often the result of taking what we know about traditional entrepreneurship and scaling enterprises and transferring it directly to social purpose organisations. While the approach originated in for-profit organising, nonprofits and their supporters often surf this wave, aiming for organisational growth as a measure of success. Taking the idea of scaling directly to mean organisational growth translates into social enterprises as growing the structure, extending the reach, increasing the number of beneficiaries served, and increasing the annual turnover. Scaling up is a quantifiable increase in the size of the organisation in terms of revenue and staff.

If you are a social entrepreneur who wants to scale your organisation's size, there are practical models and frameworks that you might find useful. For example, a textbook on social entrepreneurship by Brooks (2009) provides a linear process model that maps out the steps towards venture growth and mission success. The five clear steps can help social entrepreneurs navigate their way through a new initiative in a potentially unfamiliar context. In this commercial model, the growth of the social venture (the fourth step in the process) is equivalent to the expansion of the organisation. This approach to scaling impact is relevant when the purpose of the social enterprise is attained through the sale or provision of a product/service. Consistently, revenue growth is the name of the game. The more resources I manage, the more of this product/service I can provide, and the more impact I'll have. These growing resources might come from increased donations or subsidies, or they might come from the sales of products/services if the social enterprise funds itself through market-generated revenue (note that this doesn't imply that the organisation is for-profit as nonprofit social enterprises might also sell goods or services). And the cycle goes on. If you fund yourself with donations or subsidies, the more (measured) impact you have, the more legitimate you look in the eyes of funders, and the more additional resources you can attain to continue to grow your impact and, in turn, again, your funding. And, if you fund yourself by selling the products/services through which you have your impact, the more impact you have, the more you must have sold, and the more additional resources you have available to continue to grow your sales and impact. See the beauty of it? You might replicate the organisation in other cities, or even countries, or launch new products or services.

Box 6.2   Javier Pita, NaviLens

We decided to grow first in Spain, then Europe, the United States, and Japan because imagine if we managed to make a technology that could be used in Asia, Europe, and the United States, then we could achieve a world standard. Imagine the language and cultural barriers that we have gone through. In the end, thanks to working very hard and following the maxim that the user with visual impairment is the most important thing for us, much more important than a customer, we are achieving that growth.

So, the bigger your social enterprise, fuelled by greater revenue, the greater the positive impact, right? Often, yes, you would be right. But, not always. The clear instructions on scaling up can be reassuring, helpful, and are often linear. But they frequently don't match the reality. As much as this linear process model is helpful in providing a clear template for action, implementing a new venture is not linear, especially when it is a social enterprise (Rangan & Gregg, 2019). A social entrepreneur who tries to stick to this model may feel very disappointed and confused when the reality looks more like frequent impasses, changes in direction, and discovering unexpected opportunities that cause you to re-evaluate your approach. Also, notice how the social-political-environmental context is absent from these types of models. This is a simplified and transferable model that can be applied anywhere, which makes it useful and versatile. However, addressing a social or environmental issue usually relates to a specific location and requires deep knowledge about all the complexities of the issue that usually have a historical dimension, as well as potentially trauma, difficulties for beneficiaries, vulnerability, and other challenges. And it is important to at least be aware of these, if not address them directly.

For example, Mary is providing training and employment opportunities for young people with disabilities. If she herself has a child with disabilities, as social entrepreneurs often do have a personal connection to the social mission, then the process of setting up her organisation and delivering the service will rely on personal connections and experience and interacting with parents who have faced similar challenges. For Mary, scaling up would include either increasing the number of beneficiaries she serves or offering new services to existing beneficiaries. Finding new beneficiaries often means expanding geographically to new areas. If her social mission is to deliver a service locally, then she might think that setting up a branch of her organisation in a different country can be a good way for her to scale her impact. However, because her efficacy depends on her personal connections and experience of the issue, her "secret sauce for impact" is specific to a place, and her work or organisation might not be automatically transferable to other locations. Thus, scaling up will be challenging.

When the purpose is positive impact or social change, growing the organisation may or may not be the best way to do that. In social entrepreneurship, growing your impact requires a broader focus beyond the scope of your one organisation. Thus, growing your impact can mean influencing other organisations to support or replicate your work in other places, rather than growing your own organisation. We have found that after a period of growth, social entrepreneurs find that impact growth is limited with scaling up, and other methods are needed.

Scaling Out: Growing the Model

Social enterprises have activities that service a social/environmental mission in an innovative way. Meaning that they are not (only) delivering a service or product, but they do so through a model that is more conducive to solving the problem than pre-existing solutions. Their innovations are the result of their different, more insightful way of looking at the challenge. To end the social or environmental problem they care about, they would like others to see it in the same light they do. Thus, trying to influence broader societal practices or beliefs about it is a natural evolution of many social entrepreneurs.

Building on the example above, Mary might have successfully promoted the inclusion of people with disabilities because she has identified their particular talent. For example, some cognitively diverse people have a special talent for quality assurance-related operations. They excel where the rest of us would underperform. In that case, scaling up (growing the size of her organisation) might not be the best or quickest way to scale her mission. Instead of scaling up her organisation (or in addition to doing it), she might form new partnerships and collaborations to disseminate her ideas (van Lunenburg et al., 2020) so that more organisations working to promote the inclusion of people with disabilities can better help their beneficiaries. This scaling-out approach does not necessarily involve growing the structure of the organisation; rather, the focus is on growing the influence of the model for impact. It is the equivalent of open-source innovation.

The kinds of activities involved in scaling out differ from those involved in scaling up. Scaling out involves raising awareness of the impact of your model, reaching out to other organisations, negotiating agreements with them, and maybe training and supporting them in the first iterations while they adapt the model to their local context. Forging new collaborations with similar organisations is another way to progress a social mission. Finding new ways to disseminate your ideas and promote your mission, such as through social media, marketing campaigns, press releases, events, campaigns, webinars, or even putting up old-fashioned posters. In this case, getting copied is the name of the game. Not everybody dares explore this approach to scaling impact. If your model has become your "precious," you'll find it hard to open-source it. But this kind of Smeagol attitude is not usually the main challenge for social entrepreneurs, who are often less territorial about their solutions than traditional entrepreneurs. Because if you are prioritising a mission or some kind of social change, you are less worried about preserving a structure.

The challenge of scaling out that social entrepreneurs immediately run into is that progress is hard to measure. The social entrepreneur can find it hard to prove or show that they are making progress towards their mission, as it is hard to show how a strategic relationship has been strengthened or what part of the impact of your partners can be attributed to you. Without clear measures of progress, which are clearer in the linear scaling up approach, it is hard to proceed strategically without concrete evidence that your work is moving you towards your goals and mission.

Surely, you have already picked on the immediate other consequence of the difficulty in measuring your impact. Who pays for this? If you fund yourself with market-generated revenue, you'll have to fund it with your over-head from sales. If you fund yourself with grant funding and donations, you may have trouble obtaining it for these kinds of activities. If your funders' money is absolutely linked to the immediate outputs in beneficiaries or sales, do you have any idle resources to do this? Realistically, if you are super tight in cash for your regular activities, you'll now be thinking this is not even an option for you. This is why, often, social entrepreneurs scale up first, and once they have enough volume and, thus, bandwidth, they engage in this second approach, which they fund themselves.

Scaling Wide: Growing the Ecosystem Towards System Change

Returning to the example above, imagine that our Mary's ultimate social mission is to change societal attitudes towards people with disabilities so that employers would see them as valuable, and there would be no need for special support services like Mary's. In this case, Mary's ultimate goal is to make her organisation redundant, which is the opposite of scaling up. She would need to influence policy, practices, and societal attitudes through relationships with various actors (Lyon & Fernandez, 2012). Such activities could include deepening existing relationships and forming new strategic relationships so as to be more effective in influencing policy and practice.

Scaling wide refers to the idea of growing or progressing a social change initiative, being part of a social movement. When the organisational mission is to bring about wider social change, this is usually not caused by any one organisation in particular. In fact, it is usually a collaboration of different actors that have the real impact of social change. And the social entrepreneur sparks, orchestrates, or participates in this movement. Thus, the scaling wide approach includes scaling-out strategies – sharing ideas, collaborating with other actors with shared goals, and mapping the ecosystem – with the intention of growing or supporting the ecosystem of actors committed to the change. The ultimate goal is to change the ill-functioning system that resulted in the social/environmental problem to begin with.

As mentioned in Chapter 5, there is vast literature on social movements, but much of the learning has not fed into social entrepreneurship research and teaching. We have found in our work that practitioners often draw on social movement ideas and methods. They don't call their work "inter-disciplinary" but are simply learning from others and practically applying tools that make sense to them. In Chapter 10 we will return to the ways in which social entrepreneurs are overcoming the challenges of scaling by turning to social movement ideas. In this chapter, we highlight some of the limitations that the concept of scaling poses for social entrepreneurs with a social/environmental change mission.

A challenge of scaling wide is that while system change is often talked about, actual changes in practices, beliefs, legitimacy, and values don't happen very often and tend to take decades. In fact, this kind of change happens after violent conflict (like the spread of the concept of human rights following World War II) or other forms of huge disruption (like the end of apartheid in South Africa). But this book is not about organising uprisings; we are talking about organising for social change using innovative managerial approaches. Social entrepreneurs can aim for system change, but they do need to be realistic, patient, and realise that it is a long road.

However, as is obvious to you, dear reader, the subsequent challenge of the scaling wide approach is that there is usually no financial return and measuring impact is even more difficult than in the previous approach. Thus it becomes harder to find investors, donors, or public support. Traditional funders and investors are unlikely to fund a new and risky social change idea, especially one that is designed not to generate its own revenue but, rather, the opposite – its own disappearance.

Box 6.3   Killian Stokes, Moyee Coffee

I've yet to see a social enterprise that really has brought about systemic change. I'm always looking for an example. Patagonia. Grameen bank. So there's maybe 1 or 2. It is a tall order. Social volunteering models are brilliant – Codor dojo, Park Run – but they are not businesses. Where are all the ethical businesses, the social businesses that have brought about big change? Sometimes a woman can sit on the back of a bus and make a huge change. But that's different. It's not social entrepreneurship. Creating a positive alternative, that would be social entrepreneurship.

If you are reading this and are an impact investor, a donor, or a grant-maker, please pause and reflect. Would you be ready to fund higher order scaling out and scaling wide activities? If the answer is no, that makes you a completely average funder. If being mediocre sounds unappealing, then what changes would be necessary in your policies for you to support scaling out and scaling wide?

The Downside of Scaling

A risk of scaling is mission drift: When the effort to grow the organisation takes away from the attention given to the social mission. Social enterprise literature gives much attention to mission drift and is sometimes called "mission-market tension" (Sanders, 2015). The idea is that social entrepreneurs are working in a hybrid context, where there are competing demands between running a financially sustainable organisation and delivering maximum social impact. We like to think there is always a win-win: the better the social enterprise does financially, the more impact it can have. But this is not necessarily the case in reality. For example, if a social enterprise offers digital literacy training to youth in a disadvantaged community, it may be more financially expedient for them to focus on the simpler cases where beneficiaries do not have multiple complex issues. This approach means that more youth are served at a lower price, but it also means that the difficult cases are left behind. Thus, economic efficiency is not equivalent to increased impact.

An increasing focus on scaling social impact and social change takes its toll on the staff and volunteers and can even lead to burnout. Often social issues are stressful to deal with, and because progress isn't linear, it is easy to get discouraged. As we saw in Chapter 4, social entrepreneurs often get burnt out with the challenges of their work. An emphasis on scaling can fast track that burnout.

Box 6.4   Maria Baryamujura, COBATI

The challenge has been to fund the operations of our organisation; how do I rebuild the structures, pay salaries? How do I scale up my organisation? These are my challenges. The impact is amazing, but this all leaves me overwhelmed. When Uganda closed for COVID it was very difficult to reach our partners, tourism came to a standstill, of late domestic tourism is catching up as Ugandans especially younger people are participating in countryside adventure tours. Last year I was recognised among Africa's 100 Women Achievers in the Tourism and Travel Industry who have supported their communities in Africa. Yet, how do I get past the post-COVID pandemic challenges?

Finally, as the world of social change organising is faced with increased commercialisation (Hung & Berrett, 2022), the assumed need for scaling dominates. But, it is not always appropriate for social enterprises to scale (Bradach, 2010). The first steps involve asking whether scaling is appropriate to the social innovation or to the social enterprise (Dees et al., 2004). Many local social enterprises are delivering valuable services to their communities and fulfilling their social mission without scaling. In such cases, scaling could decrease the benefits and value that they are delivering in their community. This brings us to the question of choosing from our framework of three the right approach for the context. We will explore it later in the book.

Conclusion

In this chapter, we got down to the nitty-gritty of scaling social enterprises, unravelling the intricacies of growth through scaling up, scaling out, and scaling wide. By weaving in earlier concepts, we hope to have enhanced your comprehension of the complexities and challenges of scaling impact. The dynamic interplay between mission, strategy, and impact emphasises the need for savvy, context-specific scaling solutions in the ever-evolving arena of social ventures. In Chapter 10, we offer some guidance on how social entrepreneurs are addressing and overcoming the challenges of scaling social impact.

References

Bradach, J. L. (2010). Foreword: From scaling organizations to scaling impact. In P. N. Bloom & E. Skloot (Eds.), *Scaling social impact: New thinking* (pp. vii–xiv). Palgrave Macmillan.

Brooks, A. C. (2009). *Social entrepreneurship: A modern approach to social value creation*. Pearson Education, Inc.

Dees, J. G., Anderson, B. B., & Wei-Skillern, J. (2004). Scaling social impact: Strategies for spreading social innovations. *Stanford Social Innovation Review, 1*(4), 24–32.

Hung, C., & Berrett, J. (2022). The effects of commercialization on nonprofit efficiency and the moderating roles of government funding and organizational size. *Nonprofit Management and Leadership, 33*(4). https://doi.org/10.1002/nml.21546

Lyon, F., & Fernandez, H. (2012). Strategies for scaling up social enterprise: Lessons from early years providers. *Social Enterprise Journal, 8*(1), 63–77. https://doi.org/10.1108/17508611211226593

Rangan, V. K., & Gregg, T. (2019). How social entrepreneurs zig-zag their way to impact at scale. *California Management Review, 62*(1), 53–76.

Sanders, M. L. (2015). Being nonprofit-like in a market economy: Understanding the mission-market tension in nonprofit organizing. *Nonprofit and Voluntary Sector Quarterly, 44*(2), 205–222. https://doi.org/10.1177/0899764013508606

van Lunenburg, M., Geuijen, K., & Meijer, A. (2020). How and why do social and sustainable initiatives scale? A systematic review of the literature on social entrepreneurship and grassroots innovation. *VOLUNTAS: International Journal of Voluntary and Nonprofit Organizations, 31*(5), 1013–1024. https://doi.org/10.1007/s11266-020-00208-7

7 Ecosystems, Somewhat Unstitched

In Chapter 3, we offered you a description of what a complete ecosystem would look like, which we owe to Gonzalez and Dentchev (2021). As a quick reminder, in their study they identify three types of support for social enterprises within ecosystems: Fuel, hardware, and DNA. In a complete and well-functioning ecosystem, they intertwine in a self-reinforcing virtuous cycle. But most ecosystems aren't like that. Most ecosystems are incomplete and complex in difficult ways to trace because they have to do with the nature of each region and country, its history, and its tradition. Every place has its potentialities and also its limitations. In this chapter, we will explore some of the elements preventing ecosystems from looking like the perfect depiction many would envision.

Diversity and Dogmatism: The Odd Couple

Social entrepreneurship is a space in which people and organisations genuinely care a lot for a lot of things. If you aren't that kind of person, you won't complicate your life by trying to solve some of the most wicked problems in the world or supporting those who do. The ethical standard is very high among those who want to save the world. It almost requires being perfect sometimes. But in a varied context like social entrepreneurship, perfection according to whom? The diverse reality of social entrepreneurship is very enriching, but its value is hindered by the love of perfection that many of us close to social entrepreneurship have developed.

Someone's criteria for social entrepreneurship might not be so perfect according to someone else's criteria. This need for spotlessness makes finding each other in the middle challenging. It makes it difficult to recognise each other as social entrepreneurs, trying our very best to solve problems we care about. As discussed previously, social entrepreneurship tends to articulate in ecosystems. But, given this tendency to get along with those that very perfectly match our dogma and not so much with others that see social entrepreneurship from a different lens, articulating one powerful ecosystem that might drive the movement is proving difficult.

An example of the fragmentation of social entrepreneurship can be found in Deloitte's Global Human Capital Trends report (2018), titled "The Rise

DOI: 10.4324/9781003409694-10

of the Social Enterprise." In using the words "social enterprise," the authors refer only to for-profit social enterprises. It is perfectly reasonable to write a report that focuses on one kind of social enterprise, but the fact that they never specify that is the case makes it clear that the authors were fully unaware of large parts of the social enterprise ecosystem. This does not take away from the significance or accuracy of their findings, but it highlights how fragmented the social enterprise ecosystem is.

To engage with social enterprises, often the actors in the ecosystem need to zoom into one type of social enterprise. That in itself is not always a problem, and it is certainly necessary sometimes. For example, if I'm an impact investment fund, I will have to focus on for-profit social ventures because of the nature of the kind of support I can provide. The problem is when, in doing so, they are oblivious to the very existence of all other types. Social enterprises' support ecosystems that emerge around strict definitions and limited models hold back growth because hybridity is critical to social enterprises and a very important element of effective social entrepreneurship ecosystems (Neverauskiene & Pranskeviciute, 2021). Certain actors in the ecosystem might be better suited to support certain types of social enterprises, but the ecosystem as a whole should support them all.

But hybridity, a quintessential trait of social entrepreneurship, is why building consistent social entrepreneurship ecosystems is difficult. Social enterprise ecosystems suffer from the tension between the third and second sectors and their different institutional logics (Grassl, 2012). This tension among the players in the social enterprise world creates somewhat of a power struggle. "Power struggle! How horrible!" you might be thinking if you are a student. But if you are an experienced actor in the ecosystem, you know what we are talking about, don't you? What happens is that when there's a strong divide between sectors, social enterprises evolving from different traditions end up developing with their backs to each other and with actors in each of their ecosystems looking suspiciously at each other. This division shows up in the laws that exist or don't exist, how social enterprises and actors in the ecosystem get funding (and compete for it), government policies, informal networks, and even their overall reputation.

Box 7.1   João Magalhães, Code For All

We are for profit. So, when I'm talking to other for-profit companies, I'm the good guy. But sometimes when you are talking with owners of nonprofits, they are the good guys and all they see is you making profit. It depends on the environment where you are, and you can become easily, be the good guy and the bad guy. It's not about being a good or bad guy. It's just doing whatever it's needed to have impact and grow it.

Generating a nourishing ecosystem that can foster more social enterprises to emerge and in which already existing ones can evolve and scale is critical. Complex systems, like social enterprise ecosystems, tend to be more resilient when they have a lot of diversity among their elements, for example, when they have different actors that cater to different kinds of social enterprises. This means they can adapt better when faced with challenges and improve over time (Limburg et al., 2002). Unfortunately, in many places making such an ecosystem hybrid and inclusive is proving more challenging than a lot of actors in the ecosystem are willing to admit in public.

Intersection Challenges: Navigating Overlapping Realms

Many of the perspectives included in the broader definition of social enterprise extend beyond the boundaries of the social entrepreneurship ecosystem, connecting with distinct realms that have their own intricate ecosystems. One of its closest neighbours is the traditional entrepreneurship arena, focused on client value creation, profits, and innovation. Then, there's the social economy realm, where cooperatives, mutuals, and associations take the spotlight.

Let's look first at the overlap between social entrepreneurship and traditional entrepreneurship. The conventional entrepreneurship scene is a powerful innovation engine in countries where it is effectively articulated. Thus, the interaction between entrepreneurial ecosystems and social entrepreneurs holds significant promise for social enterprises. However, as explained by Klimas and Wronka-Pośpiech (2022), the effectiveness of this relationship can be hindered by several factors:

1. Too much homogeneity among investors within the traditional entrepreneurship ecosystem could hinder the creation and success of social ventures by limiting the chances that impact investors might emerge.
2. Stiff support organisations in the entrepreneurship ecosystem incapable of catering to social entrepreneurship might leave these ventures without essential resources, impacting their viability.
3. A lack of an altruistic culture that values both financial gain and social impact in the broader entrepreneurship ecosystem could limit the growth of social ventures.
4. Insufficient opportunities for vicarious entrepreneurial learning through which traditional entrepreneurs might learn about social venturing may hinder the emergence of successful social ventures.

Box 7.2   João Magalhães, Code For All

We had several awards in the past that were mainly for our impact. Sometimes you never know when they are taking you seriously or

> when they just saying, "nice job," but you can feel like they are not seeing you as something really serious. I only felt that respect when I was recently nominated as Entrepreneur of the Year in Portugal. I was in the 6 finalists. And I saw recognition and people approaching us with a true interest in doing business.

Another critical field overlapping this dynamic ecosystem is the movement of the social economy. The social economy is referred to as a movement that originated in the 1700s and is associated with a critique of capitalist production, unfair distribution of profits, and social inequality (Ridley-Duff & Bull, 2019). Social economy actors, as you should be able to guess by now, are not straightforward to define (sense the pattern?) but include cooperatives, mutual benefit societies, associations, foundations, nonprofits, and others. They represent a big share of many countries' economic activity and employment. For example, in the European Union (EU) there are 2.8 million social economy enterprises – that is 10% of all businesses (European Commission, 2021, December).

The social economy also faces limitations. Firstly, in some countries, social economy actors are not effectively articulated into a movement. In these cases, social enterprises with social economy models, like nonprofits, lack an organised way to relate to government or international organisations for support.

Box 7.3   Catalina Escobar, Fundación Juanfe

In Colombia, the ecosystem is lagging behind. Either we are too busy, or everyone goes their own way, I don't know. For example, there are 208,000 registered nonprofit entities in Colombia, but there is no such thing as a guild like the guild of Businesspeople. We do not have a regulatory body for the proper use and management of all that capacity.

Secondly, other countries do have important and influential ecosystem umbrella organisations, but they have varying levels of appreciation for certain for-profit approaches to social entrepreneurship. In the extreme case in which they proactively reject certain models, they might hinder the ability of social enterprises to explore various materialisations of their hybrid nature. And, as explained, limiting the diversity of social enterprises equates to limiting their ability to generate positive impact.

Navigating this intricate web of interconnected ecosystems isn't a stroll in the park. Each of these domains comes armed with its own distinct worldview, values, and priorities. Often these divisions cross the left-right political spectrum. Social entrepreneurship has been accused of, on the one hand, spreading neo-liberal beliefs and systems under the disguise of positive change, while at the same time, it has also been accused of undermining liberal globalised economic systems. So, depending on who you talk to, social entrepreneurship can be accused of one thing or its opposite. Bridging these worlds requires more than just nice words and smiles; it demands the delicate art of balancing and seeing the merit of diverse perspectives.

Public and Private Power Dynamics: It Takes Two to Tango

The different levels of public administration can be important actors in a social entrepreneurship ecosystem (Bozhikin et al., 2019):

* They can establish legal regulations and standards to ensure that social entrepreneurial organisations can operate effectively.
* They can provide financial support to social enterprises and other actors in the ecosystem through subsidies, grants, or tax incentives.
* They can foster public–private partnerships with social enterprises and other actors in the ecosystem, sharing resources and expertise with them.
* They can support social entrepreneurship through endorsing statements, media campaigns, registers for social enterprises, and labels that distinguish them.

How public and private players work together and support each other is a vital part of how an ecosystem functions in a specific country. What we find is that the power shifts between them can be quite different from one place to another. For example, social enterprise development in the United Kingdom (UK) exhibits notable variations between Scotland and England, driven by historical, political, and cultural distinctions. While both nations have shared some commonalities, including embracing Enlightenment ideals and an industrial legacy, they also possess separate legal systems and distinct political and social cultures that have influenced their social enterprise ecosystems differently.

Over the years, these disparities have grown more pronounced. In England, policies have shifted towards a market-oriented approach, reducing state support for social enterprises and encouraging private investment. In contrast, Scotland has maintained state backing for social enterprises, enacting supportive legislation. The process of devolution has further fuelled these differences, resulting in the emergence of unique social enterprise ecosystems in each region (Hazenberg, Bajwa-Patel, Roy, et al., 2016).

According to Hazenberg, Bajwa-Patel, Mazzei, et al. (2016), there are four different types of social enterprise ecosystems depending on who provides funding and how involved the government is:

- In the "Statist Macro" ecosystem, social enterprises rely heavily on national government and international institutions' funding. It's common in countries with centralised governments.
- In the "Statist Micro" ecosystem, social enterprises depend on local government policies. It's more common in decentralised states.
- The "Private Macro" ecosystem is driven mainly by private initiatives, social investment funds, and private hubs. The government doesn't provide much funding, but they enable the ecosystem through policy support and/or the creation of legal frameworks.
- In the "Private Micro" ecosystem, social enterprises don't rely much on state funding nor does government participate in creating an enabling environment. Social enterprises rely on market mechanisms and on the efforts of local associations, movements, and private funders.

You might now be left thinking, under which of these categories does my country's ecosystem fall? Hmmm . . . Maybe it's a little bit like the second, with a hint of the fourth and a bit of the first. Or maybe not. Wait, what were the four categories again? The not-so-surprising reality is that social entrepreneurship ecosystems are as hybrid and diverse as social enterprises. We put forth these categories as a helpful exercise to get your head around some of the main variables, but does that mean that every instance will perfectly fit one of your boxes? The reality is that often they won't.

Across the world, the shifting dynamics between public and private actors shape various ecosystems. If you are looking at the aseptic descriptions above and trying to decide which one you like best, you are wasting your time. Here's the catch – you can't choose your playground. The kind of ecosystem in your country will be inextricably linked to its history and administrative framework. No ecosystem ever starts from a blank slate. Much of the advice to social entrepreneurs fails to capture these differences and dynamics of ecosystems.

Governance Woes in Social Entrepreneurial Ecosystems

How much help social enterprises get from the ecosystem depends on how well the ecosystem is organised and how people work together. It's teamwork – when everyone cooperates and works together, social enterprises get a boost and more support (Diaz & Dentchev, 2021). So, as you can imagine, a usual source of stress in social enterprise ecosystems is attaining an optimal level of coordination.

As discussed above, in different countries, the role of public institutions in driving social entrepreneurship will be different. On the one hand, social entrepreneurship ecosystems can benefit from public support. However, if we think of relying only on public institutions to coordinate the ecosystem, we will need to somehow manage the potential stifling of private initiatives and public debates. In these contexts, there's a risk that networks don't get a chance to grow, and social entrepreneurs' associations must use a lot of energy in lobbying to push their own interests since there is no avenue other than the government to achieve what they might need. As a result, resources that might be made available by the private space, like hubs, incubators, and financial tools, might underdevelop. According to Neverauskiene and Pranskeviciute (2021),

> In the countries with high governance centralization and limited abilities of the society to self-organise . . . social enterprises often expect top-down incentives. Hence, in the ecosystem with a high level of governance centralization, and strong society's abilities to self-organise, the initiatives emerge in a bottom-up manner, but are fragmented and localized.

Relying too much on government as the main orchestrator of the ecosystem creates yet another governance-related challenge for social enterprises. If social enterprises and other actors supporting them are too reliant on the state, their ability to criticise and push for improvements in government responsiveness, efficiency, and integrity can be limited (Bozhikin et al., 2019). They might even loose legitimacy in front of their constituents just by being seen to be too close to public institutions. Actually, that's why some social enterprises choose not to collaborate with governments (Hsu & Jiang, 2015).

Box 7.4   Rodrigo Baggio, Recode

In Brazil, the ecosystem has grown a lot, and people have an awareness of what a social entrepreneur is. The B Corp movement has helped a lot to create awareness. So, the consciousness is there. We are seeing an evolution now in companies and wealthy families towards supporting social entrepreneurs, but there are no ecosystems created by the government. We need to create all the legal structures to create a better ecosystem for leaders of social impact. I am very committed to Catalyst in this process. We need to influence public policies.

So then we ditch government and solve the problem? Not so quickly! Firstly, we already explained the critical roles that governments at various levels can play. But, beyond that, the reality is that navigating the labyrinth of self-organisation within social entrepreneurship ecosystems, if the government isn't a central player, also poses formidable challenges. It raises profound questions about legitimacy and authority – who gets to articulate the vision for the ecosystem, and how is it achieved? The absence of a clear orchestrator often leads to a cacophony of voices, and without a unified direction, social enterprises may struggle to find their way.

In addition, finding privately founded organisations that might represent the social entrepreneurship ecosystem is not as evident everywhere. Privately managed organisations, such as professional associations, don't have the same degree of development worldwide. For example, in some countries, often coinciding with those where social entrepreneurship (at least the explicit version of it) is a relatively recent phenomenon, social entrepreneurs often feel that traditional associations need better management to enhance their activities and impact (Kabbaj et al., 2016).

In this complex landscape, the absence of a dominant governing body, be it public or private, can both liberate and confound. It liberates by fostering an environment where grassroots initiatives can flourish and where innovative ideas aren't stifled by bureaucratic constraints. Yet, it also confounds, as the absence of clear guidance can result in fragmentation and localised efforts.

Ecosystem Inequities: When Social Entrepreneurship's Resource Divide Takes a Wry Twist

Within the world of social entrepreneurship ecosystems, there's a clear and troubling divide. In prosperous cities, these ecosystems can thrive, with resources, bustling networks, and diverse forms of support. But in the most vulnerable corners of society, where people need social entrepreneurship the most, these ecosystems struggle (Todling & Wanzenbock, 2003). This unfair situation deepens inequalities and demands our immediate attention.

For example, in Mexico there's a noticeable gap between major cities like Mexico City, Monterrey, and Guadalajara and the rest of the country in terms of social entrepreneurship support (Villegas-Mateos & Vázquez-Maguirre, 2020). This leaves smaller, more remote areas with limited resources and opportunities for social entrepreneurs. In some rural communities facing significant challenges, local leaders and organisations have taken matters into their own hands (Vázquez-Maguirre, 2019). It's impressive how they have managed to build their own local support systems rooted in their core values. But it's an uphill battle for them.

The divide doesn't only operate on regional grounds. It also affects specific groups, even within the same city or region. For example, challenges persist regarding youth social entrepreneurs, often falling short of adequate support. Some young social entrepreneurs have a head start at social enterprising due to supportive family backgrounds and encouraging educational systems, but social entrepreneurship should not be restricted to a select few that enjoy these advantages. The absence of an all-encompassing ecosystem poses a formidable challenge in motivating a more extensive cohort of young individuals to embrace social entrepreneurship. Democratising this nurturing environment, rendering it accessible to a wider range of youth, represents a pressing need (Bublitz et al., 2021).

Conclusion

The challenges discussed in this chapter are not to be underestimated. How do we harness the diversity of voices to create a shared path forward? How do we engage overlapping ecosystems, like traditional entrepreneurship and social economy? How do we strike a balance between self-organisation and coordination? And perhaps most importantly, how do we ensure that resources are distributed to the most vulnerable regions and to the most pressing issues? The answers are far from straightforward. And as we weave the ecosystem, we also need to be aware of our limitations in doing it. We care a lot for a lot of things – for far too many things. If we cared a little less about fewer things, as contrary to the nature of many of us as that might be, and if we didn't need social entrepreneurship to be so "perfect" (by our standards), we would see the diversity of social entrepreneurship as the incredible strength it is. Then we might materialise the potential of social entrepreneurship as an amazing movement that can change the way in which we tackle social and environmental problems. "Social entrepreneurship" is a reality of which no one can claim ownership. And that is great.

References

Agarwal, D., Bersin, J., Lahiri, G., Schwartz, J., & Volini, E. (2018). *The rise of the social enterprise: 2018 Deloitte global human capital trends.* Deloitte Insights.

Bozhikin, I., Macke, J., & da Costa, L. F. (2019). The role of government and key non-state actors in social entrepreneurship: A systematic literature review. *Journal of Cleaner Production, 226,* 730–747.

Bublitz, M. G., Chaplin, L. N., Peracchio, L. A., Cermin, A. D., Dida, M., Escalas, J. E., & Miller, E. G. (2021). Rise up: Understanding youth social entrepreneurs and their ecosystems. *Journal of Public Policy & Marketing, 40*(2), 206–225.

European Commission. (2021, December). *Factsheet.* https://ec.europa.eu/social/main.jsp?langId=en&catId=89&newsId=10117&furtherNews=yes#navItem-1

Gonzalez, A. D., & Dentchev, N. A. (2021). Ecosystems in support of social entrepreneurs: A literature review. *Social Enterprise Journal, 17*(3), 329–360.

Grassl, W. (2012). Business models of social enterprise: A design approach to hybridity. *ACRN Journal of Entrepreneurship Perspectives, 1*(1), 37–60.

Hazenberg, T., Bajwa-Patel, M., Mazzei, M. J., & Baglioni, S. (2016). The role of institutional and stakeholder networks in shaping social enterprise ecosystems in Europe. *Social Enterprise Journal, 12*(3), 302–321.

Hazenberg, R., Bajwa-Patel, M., Roy, M. J., Mazzei, M., & Baglioni, S. (2016). A comparative overview of social enterprise "ecosystems" in Scotland and England: An evolutionary perspective. *International Review of Sociology*, *26*(2), 205–222.

Hsu, C. L., & Jiang, Y. (2015). An institutional approach to Chinese NGOs: State alliance versus state avoidance resource strategies. *China Quarterly*, *221*, 100e122. https://doi.org/10.1017/S0305741014001568

Kabbaj, M., El Ouazzani Ech Hadi, K. H. A. L. I. D., Elamrani, J., & Lemtaoui, M. (2016). A study of the social entrepreneurship ecosystem: The case of Morocco. *Journal of Developmental Entrepreneurship*, *21*(4), 1650021.

Klimas, P., & Wronka-Pośpiech, M. (2022). Social entrepreneurship and entrepreneurial ecosystems: Do they fit? *Problemy Zarządzania*, *20*(1(95)), 43–66.

Limburg, K. E., O'Neill, R. V., Costanza, R., & Farber, S. (2002). Complex systems and valuation. *Ecological Economics*, *41*(3), 409–420.

Neverauskiene, L. O., & Pranskeviciute, I. (2021). Hybridity of social enterprise models and ecosystems. *Journal of International Studies*, *14*(1).

Ridley-Duff, R., & Bull, M. (2019). *Understanding social enterprise: Theory and practice* (3rd ed.). Sage Publishing.

Todling, F., & Wanzenbock, H. (2003). Regional differences in structural characteristics of start-ups. *Entrepreneurship and Regional Development*, *15*(4), 351–370.

Vázquez-Maguirre, M. (2019). El desarrollo sostenible a través de empresas sociales en comunidades indígenas de América Latina. *Estudios Sociales*, *29*(53), 2–22.

Villegas-Mateos, A., & Vázquez-Maguirre, M. (2020). Social entrepreneurial ecosystems: A regional perspective of Mexico. *International Journal of Entrepreneurship*, *24*(1), 1–19.

Part 3

The Potential

8 Social Value Creators

Accepting Vulnerability and Nurturing Well-Being for Impact

As much as we would like for social entrepreneurs to resemble the Tony Starks and Wonder Women of the impact world, we can't expect them to fit this mould. The passion and purpose that drive social entrepreneurs to make positive changes can also take a toll on them. Indeed, passion and purpose are the fires that ignite change. Yet, these very flames can consume the well-being of individuals and teams. Let's remember some fundamental challenges:

1. **Self-Care and Vulnerability:** Social entrepreneurs are not invincible. The relentless demands, the mounting pressure, and the emotional toll they bear are significant.
2. **Community and Team Dynamics:** While the hero narrative often zooms in on individual leaders, have you contemplated the immense role that communities and teams play in social entrepreneurship? Their diversity and dynamics can drive or hinder social change.
3. **Decision-Making Pitfalls:** Embracing diversity means acknowledging the pitfalls that come with various leadership styles. No Social entrepreneur possesses infallible decision-making skills.
4. **Alienation and Inclusivity:** The narrative of social entrepreneurs as one-in-a-million heroes can be alienating to those who don't see themselves as such. Have you ever questioned the exclusivity of this narrative?

Let's delve into the art of self-preservation and collective empowerment in the world of social entrepreneurship.

Fostering Self-Care and Well-Being: The Balancing Act

Truth is, it's easy for social entrepreneurs to lose themselves in the pursuit of their mission. When dreams of transformative impact burn brightly, crossing the line into workaholic territory happens almost inadvertently. But imagine you're pouring from a cup, one fed with your drive, energy, and health – it can't be empty. In a field marked by commendable goals, remembering that social entrepreneurs are susceptible to burnout is essential. When you are

DOI: 10.4324/9781003409694-12

involved in trying to solve critical problems, self-care is not just a luxury; it's an absolute necessity.

Of course, if you are a social entrepreneur managing a growing organisation, you might now be thinking: "If that was only possible." You start work in the morning, and responsibilities mount up – fundraising, attending meetings, interviewing candidates, and so on. Your day looks much like any office administrator's, only with a much higher emotional burden and less funding. And you know all this is necessary to continue to help solve the social/environmental challenges you set yourself to confront. So what to do?

Box 8.1   Catalina Escobar, Fundación Juanfe

My family instilled in me that you must work and work and otherwise, you were not good enough. I had no Saturdays or Sundays, and I felt very proud of living like that. But in 2018 everything came crashing down on me and I went into a depression. I learned to delegate. And I started to go on vacation, disconnect the phone; I exercise and like to read. I realised that if I'm not well, I wasn't going to solve anything for the girls we support at Juanfe.

"Balance" would be the watchword here. On the one hand, you should explore the recommendations that every person should keep in mind regarding physical activity, healthy eating habits, sleep, and mindfulness. There are many books written about them by people who are much more expert in these fields than we are, so we won't expand on this and just recommend that you learn and, more importantly, apply their advice. But, focusing on what is specific to social entrepreneurship, let's not forget that this emotional toll results from the great purpose that drives your work. And here you, as someone involved in social entrepreneurship, have an additional headspring of wellbeing that not everyone has so readily available. Daily tasks might keep you from seeing firsthand the impact of what you do. Many social entrepreneurs who find themselves in this kind of situation make a point of building opportunities for field work regularly. This will take different forms for different people in different projects, but that connection with the natural environment you are helping protect or the people you are supporting will give you the necessary energy to troop through the less exciting tasks you need to do.

This connects with another one of the things that help social entrepreneurs be happier about their daily work: The possibility of having more say in the tasks they perform (Kibler et al., 2019). Alright, you can't simply ditch all these things that are on your to-do list just to do whatever it is that you enjoy the most, among other reasons, because partners often require the top management in the organisations to be the ones at those meetings. But, by prioritising time in the field, you will keep that sense of having some freedom in what you do within the limits of what is your responsibility.

Box 8.2   João Magalhães, Code For All

Reaching milestones, growing, and getting awards were great achievements. But even today, when I need to get energy, I go and I just speak with some of our students that are doing a course right now, and they tell me about their stories, and that's really inspiring. Some are changing their lives completely. They are why we get through tough moments.

The previous strategy, as straightforward as it might seem, is of great help to some social entrepreneurs. But let's not forget that diverse individuals bring diverse needs. There are specific triggers that can elevate the likelihood of burnout, making it a substantial problem that might require additional emotional scaffolding:

- Dealing with traumatic issues: Social entrepreneurs who tackle issues that are inherently traumatic, such as addiction, or sexual abuse, face a greater risk of burnout. Constant exposure to traumas associated with such issues can lead to secondary traumatic stress, further increasing the chances of burnout.
- Personal connection to the cause: When your work originates from your personal experiences, drawing the line between professional and personal life is close to impossible, which can increase the likelihood of emotional exhaustion. Now imagine the emotional toll if that personal experience is a traumatic one as those described above.
- Dealing with systemic issues: Many social issues are related to historic, societal, cultural, or in short, systemic issues (think racism, misogyny, discrimination, and poverty). These are particularly intractable, as they are often unseen, taken-for-granted, or part of our unconscious biases. When any individual takes on a systemic issue, it is a David and Goliath situation – systemic issues are simply too big for any one individual to take on. And worse, systemic issues are often pathologised as individual problems, making the challenge hard to articulate or recognise.

By acknowledging the specific challenges associated with personal connections to the cause and dealing with traumatic and systemic issues, social entrepreneurs and their support systems can take proactive steps to safeguard their well-being and long-term impact. For some, self-care may involve regular visits to the very communities they serve, while for others, it may also mean seeking therapy, ideally preventively. Regardless of the form, self-care is the cornerstone of resilience.

Creating self-nourishing rituals and habits is important, but it tends not to be urgent until you are deep in trouble. It might always feel like there is something more important to do. In this context, radical self-care can be the name of the game. Can self-care be radical? Can it be a form of rebellion? As an interesting example of radical self-care, we would like to bring to your attention the Nap Ministry (this is real; look it up!). A radical advocate for rest, the Nap Ministry champions the idea that rest is a form of rebellion in a society glorifying perpetual toil. Self-care and rest are not concessions; they are strategies for longevity, yours and that of the social enterprise you are involved in. It's a message that challenges the status quo and drives home the urgency of permanently recharging.

If you are involved in social entrepreneurship, this might be a good moment to ask yourself, what does self-care mean to you in your social entrepreneurial journey? How do you see it as the cornerstone of resilience and sustainability? Self-care is not a sign of weakness; it's a demonstration of wisdom and commitment to continuing to work in the long run on the matters you care for, as personal, traumatic, and/or systemic they might be. Setting boundaries and cultivating self-nurturing practices are signs of a strategic mindset.

Box 8.3   Rodrigo Baggio, Recode

If you follow your dreams and passions and invest time and enthusiasm, and see your dreams materialise, social entrepreneurship is an amazing way to be happy and help change the world for the better. It is a great thing to do. But keeping your wellbeing, your health, managing your life, this is important for your results. We tell our students in Recode to operate at three levels: First, at a personal level with your family in a regenerative lifestyle. The second level is the organisational or cause level – in my case Recode – which is my mission. But the third level is everyone, that I try to affect through Catalyst and other initiatives. It is the most associative way to change the system, to orchestrate change. If we move in the three, we impact better.

Firm-Level Well-Being and Effectiveness: Team Resilience

Social entrepreneurship isn't only about being purposeful and committed; it's about being competent in confronting the problems you set yourself to tackle. One critical element to this is effectively managing the team involved in the social enterprise. As mentioned before, teams, volunteers, and the broader community play a paramount role in the success of social enterprises. It's a shame how this obvious fact flies under the radar so often.

In systems theory, it is clear that higher levels of a system only make sense in order to serve lower levels of the system and make sure they can achieve their purpose (Meadows, 2008). You can think about it as a pyramid in which the really important work happens on the ground floor and all other levels exist to serve that most impactful one. In the case of a social enterprise that is growing, the leadership does not generate the impact directly. The leadership's role is to create the environment that makes it possible for their team to generate impact.

If you lead or are in the management of a social enterprise, bringing together the right team, supporting their well-being, and making sure that they are led professionally and transparently are among your key responsibilities. As Uncle Ben told Peter Parker in *Spiderman* "With great power comes great responsibility" (you might not feel that you have "great" power, but you get the point). Or, to quote an academic paper, "Although it is commonly suggested that power corrupts, the data tell a different story: power reveals. When leaders gain power, they have the freedom and resources to express their values" (Bolino & Grant, 2016). Are you truly committed to solving a certain environmental/social problem? Then that should be very visible in the way in which you manage the team that is indeed solving it.

Proactively managing the team can be especially important in the case of social enterprises because they are in a league of their own when it comes to recruiting and keeping talent. They need to balance both business/management savvy and social sector smarts, both of which are essential to attain their mission (Liu & Ko, 2012). You must appreciate and proactively orchestrate all these diverse talents to advance your mission.

Box 8.4   João Magalhães, Code For All

When there's a team of 10 people or a team with 50 or 100, 200, we are now close to 300, you need to change the way you manage the organisation. As you grow, the culture becomes very important, because in social enterprises, we have people much more looking into impact. And we have other people much more focused on scaling. And you need both of them because that's the way you build something special. But it's also challenging to have a balance.

As we discussed earlier in this book, you can't just assume team dynamics and well-being are taken care of by the fact that they do "such pretty work" and they are "so committed." Citizenship fatigue and the more profound compassion fatigue are very real. Team building is paramount for achieving success in social enterprise teams. The probability of citizenship fatigue significantly lowers among employees when social entrepreneurs cultivate robust, positive connections with their team members and among them (Bolino et al., 2015). These strong team bonds enhance collaboration, boost morale, and promote a shared commitment to the organisation's mission. Spending time in team building activities clearly pays off in the well-being of the team and in the form of sustained commitment towards impact.

Everyone involved in the social enterprise benefits, just like the leaders, from remaining connected to the positive value of their work. Of course, the closer the person is to the real impact, the more connected they might already be with it. But, at the same time, sometimes the trees don't let you see the forest and the daily struggles might make them lose sight of the overall positive impact. Making sure that they are exposed to that overall impact and all the positive stories about it is paramount. Research underscores that beneficiaries better convey messages of a prosocial impact to the team than the social enterprises' leaders (Grant & Hofmann, 2011). Their stories make the impact tangible. However, employees perceived the prosocial impact most when both leaders and beneficiaries conveyed the message: Leaders painted the big picture of how the work benefits others, and beneficiaries made it personal (Grant, 2012).

In addition, within social enterprises' teams, wellness initiatives also wield tremendous power. Employees and/or volunteers might be tempted just to quit if they can't see a way to make their work compatible with their well-being. The motto "Rest, don't quit" is so trite we have even found T-shirts with it. You might want to get a few for your team right after creating the strategies for them to, indeed, rest physically and emotionally. Mental health support might be another cog in the machinery of well-being for some in especially emotionally demanding positions. For example, when dealing with trauma and abuse, team members need more than just accolades; they need a haven for healing. Often, more so than the leaders of the social enterprises since the team members are usually the ones doing the frontline work. We must recognise that their work bears emotional weight and offer the scaffolding of mental health resources.

Another situation that calls for special attention to team dynamics is when social enterprises accelerate their scale. Scaling a social enterprise heralds growth and challenges in equal measure. Balancing professional management with personal support becomes paramount. Clear Terms of Reference (TORs) and performance metrics are critical. As the team burgeons, the impact of decisions takes on greater proportions. You can create real damage both by shifting too quickly into goal-oriented management if your team isn't used to it, thus neglecting the human element, and by trying to keep very informal, relationship-based human resource management that can lead to very unfair situations due to a lack of accountability.

For example, as you scale the team the potential impact on others of the social entrepreneur protecting someone who is clearly underperforming because they are friends, or because they have been in the organisation for many years, is greater. Depending on your values and on your impact (maybe this person belongs to the community whose employability you are trying to foster), you need a proactively planned strategy to manage such situations that is clear and transparent. It might take the form of a flexible plan to help the person transition out of the organisation or a clear policy explaining under what circumstances people will get fired even if they are beneficiaries or transparently explaining that they never will and then bearing with the consequences as part of the role of the social enterprise.

Box 8.5   Catalina Escobar, Fundación Juanfe

We learned that social impact bonds for employment were in the making in Colombia. They pay for the results, and we have results. The final payer was public, but the initial financier assuming the risk was missing, and we decided to be both operator and financier. We were the first foundation in Latin America to trade on the Stock Exchange, like Ford Foundation does in the USA. We achieved the financing goal in two and a half minutes. This is incredible, but to achieve it, you must lead a very professional organisation.

An additional challenge that social enterprises face is that of knowing when to shift course from failing strategies which, as we discussed previously in the book, are stickier in the case of prosocial organisations. Solving this problem requires self-awareness on the part of everyone involved and the utilisation of an effective impact measurement system. Self-awareness doesn't always come easily. It is not a matter of just telling people to "be more self-aware." You need to create an environment that is conducive to it. Self-awareness can be engineered by creating specific opportunities/processes/rituals for constructive criticism and feedback within the team and among the team and the leadership. This must be proactively encouraged as a critical tool in refining their strategies and realigning their efforts with their overarching goals.

In later chapters, we will talk more thoroughly about impact, but let's just highlight here that one of its main benefits is aligning the team and avoiding ill-informed group dynamics that might lead to stubbornly committing to initiatives that aren't delivering the expected impact. The ability to recognise when a particular approach is not working and having the courage to adjust is essential for achieving lasting success. Beyond frequent internal feedback, external evaluations also provide an objective perspective on the effectiveness of a social enterprise's initiatives. These assessments offer valuable insights into what is working and what isn't, helping teams make informed decisions.

Structural Support: An Ecosystem That Recognises That Not All Heroes Wear Capes

Social entrepreneurship comes with a mosaic of experiences, backgrounds, and visions. Within this diverse tapestry, leaders of social enterprises are not superhuman, nor should we expect them to be. Have you ever thought about what happens when you strip away the hero's cape and see the person beneath? You'll find that leaders of social enterprises are more Clark Kent than Superman. By recognising the vulnerability of those involved in social entrepreneurship, we pave the way for a more inclusive and supportive ecosystem.

The different organisations in the social entrepreneurship ecosystem should support self-care in the social entrepreneurship landscape. Investors, funders, policymakers, and others should understand that social entrepreneurs are not perpetual motion machines. The path to societal transformation requires rest stops. Otherwise, it's like running a marathon without water stations. To preserve the vitality of social entrepreneurs, this ecosystem must provide the essential refuelling points.

Box 8.6   Rodrigo Baggio, Recode

I started with some friends an initiative to do peer exchange groups for social impact leaders to make it possible for them to talk about the most important things in their lives on a personal and professional level in a self-supporting cycle. We now have around 31 groups in partnership with Catalyst. We need to find ways to reconnect with our passion and soul.

All actors in the ecosystem need to work together to create an enabling environment for social entrepreneurs to take care of themselves and their teams, rather than celebrate their martyrdom. This is contrary to participating in the culture, generalised in some regions of the world much more than in others, that celebrates continuous exhaustion as a sign of commitment or success. Please pause and ponder for a second how absurd the way some people brag about their exhaustion as if it were a sign of their importance. They boast of being drained (they try to make it sound like a complaint, but you know they are basically telling you how important they are), and others admire them, wishing to be equally "successfully destroyed" as some kind of badge of accomplishment. How did lacking any ability to care for yourself become a synonym for being successful in the minds of so many people? If you've read this last paragraph and didn't relate at all, good for you! You probably live in a much healthier culture than others in certain professional spaces.

It is also surprising how often actors in the ecosystem lose sight of the importance of proactively supporting and engaging with the teams/volunteers working in the social enterprises they are so fond of supporting and/or the communities in which they operate. In Light's words:

> The second bias that comes from focusing on individuals is a tendency to ignore the role of organisations and the resources they provide for pattern-breaking change. Researchers have long known that successful ideas require a mix of talents that is rarely found in one person. Indeed, the most compelling research on business entrepreneurship suggests that successful change requires a stream of capabilities including leadership, management, marketing, organisational design, and finance. Whereas philanthropists almost always focus on the individual, venture capitalists almost always focus on the leadership team and the organisation to back it.
>
> (Light, 2006, p. 48)

To all you investors, donors, and supporters of social entrepreneurs, here's some additional food for thought. It might be time to start building well-being initiatives into your funding if you aren't doing it already. It might be time to ask the organisations you support to report on their talent management and well-being efforts – for their staff and the people driving their missions. If we're serious about making lasting change and scaling up our impact, it starts with the well-being of the people who are on the frontlines, making it all happen.

Box 8.7   Catalina Escobar, Fundación Juanfe

I've been in this for twenty-two years. I demanded a lot from myself, travelled a lot, and suffered to make time for my children and not damage my motherhood. I cried a lot, and it was very hard. I now realise that sometimes I put unnecessary pressure on myself. We must let go of some worries. You must have a healthy mind in a healthy body and thus maintain the ability to lead and move others. I would say to the social entrepreneur who starts: work very hard, but take care of yourself and don't obsess so much about the short-term result. We want everything now, and change takes time.

Conclusion

Consider a shift in perspective where the central figures in this narrative are not all-powerful heroes but rather a diverse group of people, with their personal stories and vulnerabilities, undertaking gargantuan tasks. For them, self-care is not a luxury but a necessity. Social entrepreneurs must take proactive steps, including regular field visits, striving for a balanced approach to work and life, peer support, or therapy. We also stressed the importance of proactive team management in social entrepreneurship, through team building, positive connections, and creating an environment that encourages constructive feedback. To bring about lasting change, all actors in the ecosystem must collaborate in creating an enabling environment for self-care. Let's appreciate that social entrepreneurs don't wear a suit of armour; they tend to be more comfortable in casual attire.

References

Bolino, M. C., & Grant, A. M. (2016). The bright side of being prosocial at work, and the dark side, too: A review and agenda for research on other-oriented motives, behavior, and impact in organizations. *Academy of Management Annals, 10*(1), 599–670.

Bolino, M. C., Hsiung, H. H., Harvey, J., & LePine, J. A. (2015). "Well, I'm tired of tryin'!" Organizational citizenship behavior and citizenship fatigue. *Journal of Applied Psychology, 100*(1), 56.

Grant, A. M. (2012). Leading with meaning: Beneficiary contact, prosocial impact, and the performance effects of transformational leadership. *Academy of Management Journal, 55*(2), 458–476.

Grant, A. M., & Hofmann, D. A. (2011). Outsourcing inspiration: The performance effects of ideological messages from leaders and beneficiaries. *Organizational Behavior and Human Decision Processes, 116*(2), 173–187.

Kibler, E., Wincent, J., Kautonen, T., Cacciotti, G., & Obschonka, M. (2019). Can prosocial motivation harm entrepreneurs' subjective well-being? *Journal of business venturing, 34*(4), 608–624.

Light, P. C. (2006). Reshaping social entrepreneurship. *Stanford Social Innovation Review, 4*(3), 47–51.

Liu, G., & Ko, W. W. (2012). Organizational learning and marketing capability development: A study of the charity retailing operations of British social enterprise. *Nonprofit and Voluntary Sector Quarterly, 41*(4), 580–608.

Meadows, D. H. (2008). *Thinking in systems: A primer*. Chelsea Green Publishing.

9 From Reporting to Revolution

Choosing Your Social Impact Lens

In Chapter 5 we saw an array of drawbacks and problems with social impact measurement:

- We often see outcomes reported instead of impact, which may be more realistic anyway.
- Impact measurement is often donor driven and a burden on the organisation (prioritising accountability over organisational learning).
- There are problems of attribution (is the impact due to your work?) and causation (is there a clear causal link between the action and the impact?) that undermine the social entrepreneurs' ability to convincingly report on impact.
- Social change? Social impact measurement can emphasise measurable aspects of organising, whereas the social enterprise may be motivated by a bigger social change that can be overlooked by impact measurement tools and reporting.
- The legitimacy paradox: Social change involves changing societal beliefs, values, and practices. Social entrepreneurs need legitimacy to operate, but their missions don't operate within spaces that fit with current societal attitudes and beliefs.

Box 9.1   Javier Pita, NaviLens

Measuring impact is often problematic. Because, what is really important? You measure numbers of users, but to what degree of use? Or talking about expansion, for example, NaviLens is being used right now in 138 countries. And you say wow, okay, that's spectacular. I think it's spectacular. But of course, does that really comfort us or do we have to achieve that a blind person in any country can be completely independent in their day to day? How do you measure that? Social impact is often more like an abstraction, than a quantification.

DOI: 10.4324/9781003409694-13

Literature and practice provide insights into how to deal with these impact challenges. There are no simple answers, but there are different approaches we can take that help address the problems. We advise donors and practitioners to distinguish between three different approaches to impact that operate at three levels from micro to macro. Impact measurement as:

1. A reporting framework (micro-level).
2. A management tool for organisational learning and strategic development (meso-level).
3. A compass guiding the broader societal change you hope to bring about (macro-level).

A reporting framework: Here the social entrepreneur can apply some of the many tools and frameworks with the purpose of improved accountability and accurate precise reporting. Often the framework consists of reporting guidelines directed by donors or investors. Imagine social impact measurement as a finely crafted microscope, honed in on the nitty-gritty details of your impact initiatives. At its core, this approach is like the forensic expert of the impact world, zooming in to uncover accountability with surgical precision. Through the lens of micro-level social impact measurement, organisations can track the details of their activities, pinpoint exactly what changes they're making, identify who is benefiting, and how these changes connect to their mission. It's a game of transparency, helping build trust with stakeholders, and showing them that every cent and kilogram of effort is accounted for. Impact reporting in this approach can be quantified and links up well with the auditing and accounting tradition that we saw in Chapter 3.

A management tool for organisational learning and strategic development: Impact measurement can serve as a regular practice for a social enterprise, the results of which shape the organisation's activities and strategic planning. Think of this approach as a coach who not only evaluates your performance but also helps you evolve and strategise for the future. It's your organisational mirror, reflecting back your strengths and weaknesses. Think of it as a perpetual improvement cycle. Impact measurement becomes a regular exercise that informs strategic planning and influences everyday activities. With this approach, organisations can embrace a culture of learning and adaptation. The feedback loop is the key. It's not just about proving your impact but understanding how to enhance it. It's about constantly refining your strategies, fine-tuning your methods, and sharpening your impact like a well-crafted blade.

A compass guiding social change: Now, let's take a step back and envision impact measurement as a guiding star in the night sky, leading social enterprises on their epic journey. When a social enterprise has an overarching social change that drives the organisation or the individual, social impact can serve as a compass guiding the priorities and direction. This is the visionary approach, the North Star, and the compass that keeps you on the path of social change. Sometimes, impact measurement can be so focused on the trees that it forgets about the forest. Social entrepreneurs may have grand visions of societal change, but these broader goals can get lost in the metrics and numbers. This is where the macro-level approach shines. Social impact here serves as a compass, guiding organisations towards the bigger social change they aspire to bring about. It helps them align their day-to-day activities with their grand mission. With this approach, organisations can tackle the legitimacy paradox head-on. By keeping their eyes on the societal transformation that they aim to achieve, they can engage with current societal attitudes and beliefs in a way that makes them relevant and credible. It's like painting a masterpiece small brushstroke at a time while never losing sight of the grand canvas.

In the world of social impact measurement, these three approaches are not tools; they're lenses, each offering a unique perspective on the same mosaic of creating a better world. In fact, one organisation can use all three of these lenses or any one of them. Whether you're diving into the micro-details, orchestrating meso-level improvements, or following the macro-level North Star, the key is to adapt and choose the approach that best fits your mission. After all, changing the world is no easy task, but with these three lenses, you'll have a clearer view of how to get there. Below we explore how to implement all three, and then how to choose the lens that fits your mission.

How to Implement the Three Lenses of Social Impact

Let's explore how a social enterprise can effectively implement all three approaches to social impact measurement. Imagine a fictional social enterprise called "GreenSolutions" that focuses on environmental conservation and community development. Here's how GreenSolutions can put these approaches into action:

Social Impact as a Reporting Framework (Micro-Level): GreenSolutions can start by defining clear and measurable indicators of its environmental and community impact. For example:

- **Environmental Impact:** Measure the number of trees planted, reduction in carbon emissions, and improved air and water quality in target areas.
- **Community Impact:** Track improvements in the livelihoods of local communities, such as increased income, access to education, and healthcare.

Implementation Steps:

1. **Define the Scope of the Impact:** Establish the geographic or sectorial boundaries and the stakeholders to be considered, such as how to define

who the members of the local communities are exactly or what the frontiers of the target area are where you will measure air quality.

2. **Develop a Theory of Change:** Following the model already presented in Chapter 5, craft the complete causal chain that will connect your activities with the impact you are trying to create. For example, how does this particular training eventually result in improved livelihoods and better water quality?

3. **Select Key Performance Indicators (KPIs):** Identify the specific metrics that align with GreenSolutions' mission, such as the number of trees planted per month or the percentage increase in community income.

4. **Data Collection and Analysis:** Establish data collection methods, whether through surveys, field assessments, or collaborations with local partners. Analyse the data to track progress.

5. **Regular Reporting:** Create periodic reports that highlight the results and share them with stakeholders, including donors, investors, and the local community.

6. **Transparency and Accountability:** GreenSolutions can ensure that it transparently reports its progress, highlighting both successes and challenges.

Social Impact as a Management Tool for Organisational Learning and Strategic Development (Meso-Level): To enhance its impact, GreenSolutions can use impact measurement as a tool for organisational growth and development. In this approach, you would replicate steps 1–4 described previously, but what you do with the information is different. You don't gather the information to report it; you gather it to learn and improve. So, the result of implementing steps 1–4 with this other goal in mind might change.

Implementation Steps (after implementing steps 1–4 above):

1. **Continuous Feedback Loop:** Develop a culture of learning by regularly reviewing the impact data. Use this feedback to make informed decisions.

2. **Strategic Planning:** Integrate impact data into the organisation's strategic planning process. For instance, if the data show that certain tree planting methods are more effective, adjust strategies accordingly.

3. **Capacity Building:** Invest in staff training and development to improve data collection, analysis, and interpretation skills.

4. **Iterative Improvement:** Encourage experimentation and innovation based on insights gained from impact measurement. For example, if the data suggest that involving local communities more in tree planting activities has a greater impact, GreenSolutions can adapt its approach accordingly.

Social Impact as a Compass Guiding Social Change (Macro-Level): GreenSolutions can use impact measurement as a guiding compass to stay aligned with its long-term vision for social and environmental change. This is yet another use of the information gathered, and once more, the defined use will condition what information needs to be gathered and how it is done.

Implementation Steps:

1. **Define the Grand Mission:** Clearly articulate the broader societal changes GreenSolutions aims to achieve, such as reforestation of entire regions, poverty reduction, and sustainable development. This will be reflected in GreenSolutions' Theory of Change, and it might require enlarging the scope of the impact, the relevant stakeholder, and geographic boundaries.
2. **Alignment with Mission:** Regularly evaluate all activities against this mission. Ask if each action contributes to the overarching social change goals. And, consequentially, cut back those that don't or are less effective in doing so to focus resources on those that most contribute to the grand mission.
3. **Community Engagement:** Involve the local community in shaping and executing the mission, ensuring it resonates with their needs and aspirations. Their input can be invaluable in adapting and evolving your activities over time to remain relevant and boost impact in the face of ever-changing circumstances.
4. **Advocacy and Alliances:** Use the compass of social impact to advocate for policy changes, and establish alliances with other organisations and institutions working towards similar social changes.

By using all three approaches in conjunction, GreenSolutions can ensure that its impact measurement efforts not only hold the organisation accountable but also drive continuous improvement and align the enterprise with its grand mission. This holistic approach empowers GreenSolutions to be more effective in making a lasting positive impact on both the environment and the communities it serves.

Box 9.2   Killian Stokes, Moyee Coffee

One of the farmers said to me, the multinationals have been here for 20 years, and nothing has changed for the farmers. And that is where I get angry. I don't just want to be ticking a box, so I can go and promote an ethical coffee company, so I can say oh here's a social entrepreneur. And I don't want to do that if it's not making a damn difference, you know? . . . We've grown organically over the past seven years, you know bootstrapping. We didn't take any major loans, just a line of credit for the coffee beans. Lots of businesses went bust during Covid; we survived and have a staff of eight. We went from a blank sheet of paper to supplying Google EMEA headquarters with their coffee, and we support 10,000 farmers. We've helped build a roastery, and create a model farm, help pay farmers bonuses. 10,000 farmers in three countries are getting paid decently for their coffee. And we're buying that coffee and selling it to our clients here.

Selecting One Lens: Levels of Social Change

Alternatively, a social enterprise may be better placed to select one of these three lenses. How to select which one is right for your organisation brings us to the concept of levels of social change. As mentioned (briefly) in Chapter 5, a recognised typology of social entrepreneurs helps us to analyse three different levels of social change: Social bricoleurs work at a local level to bring about incremental change, social constructionists work at a meso-level (national, regional) to take advantage of new opportunities for social change interventions, and social engineers aim to bring about more macro-level system change (Zahra et al., 2009). While this framework relates to social entrepreneurs, when considering organisations, we have found that often there is an evolution from new social enterprises that start out with local-level incremental initiatives to young organisations that have developed their idea to become a more serious social change intervention, to mature organisations that are trying to bring about significant social change often on a larger geographic scale. The size of the organisation does not necessarily correspond with these three levels. A large organisation can be delivering a local social service, while a small organisation can be working towards a significant system change or change in legitimacy and societal practices.

Box 9.3   Maria Baryamujura, COBATI

I see my impact in terms of social change, not just numbers. Imagine a scenic area, lakes in the background, and then in the middle, at a rural homestead they are preparing traditional food. They have everything, but they are poor. All they need is to realise that their environment and culture are worthy. Their culture is embedded in their way of life, the handcraft of their women, their food, stories. They usually think about survival every day. But mentor, inspire, and train them, build their confidence to look further, talk about saving and investing, create a mindset shift. Sometimes people get to the communities and want to pay less. At a hotel they get junk food and willingly pay more. But at a community homestay they expect to pay little for products that are organic and of higher quality. My work is much more about empowering people living in the countryside to be confident enough about the fact that their culture, heritage, indigenous knowledge, food, and open-air green environment, are all valuable and can give them many streams of income without leaving their villages.

Below we elaborate on how social entrepreneurs and their organisations can select the appropriate approach to social impact measurement according to the three lenses: Micro, meso, and macro. This will depend on the age of the organisation and/or the degree of social change they aim to achieve and/or their specific social mission.

Micro-Level Approach (Social Impact as a Reporting Framework):

- **Organisation Age/New Organisations:** If you are a young organisation with limited resources, focusing on a micro-level approach is suitable. It helps maintain transparency and accountability without overwhelming your capacity.
- **Degree of Social Change/Incremental Change:** For organisations aiming for incremental change in specific areas, the micro-level approach is effective. It allows you to demonstrate and communicate tangible, short-term results. Often social enterprises start out with an incremental change mandate, and as they evolve, they begin more and more to work towards more systemic change. Zahra et al. call these changemakers "social bricoleurs" as they bring together resources in new ways for local initiatives. They often evolve into more significant social change efforts.
- **Specific Social Mission/Service Delivery:** If your mission primarily revolves around delivering straightforward services, such as providing meals to the homeless, the micro-level approach is ideal. It allows you to showcase measurable outputs and outcomes.

Meso-Level Approach (Social Impact as a Management Tool):

- **Organisation Age/Young Organisations:** Young but not new organisations with more resources and capacity can effectively use impact measurement as a management tool. It fosters a culture of learning and adaptation, leading to strategy improvement.
- **Degree of Social Change/Moderate Change:** Organisations seeking moderate social change can benefit from this approach. It enables them to continuously learn and adapt based on data, optimising their strategies for more substantial impact. Zahra et al. (2009) call these change agents "social constructionists," those who aim to take advantage of opportunities to increase their impact.
- **Specific Social Mission/Hybrid Missions:** Organisations with hybrid missions, encompassing both service delivery and broader social change, can find value in the meso-level approach. It allows them to improve their services while also making strides towards larger societal goals.

Macro-Level Approach (Social Impact as a Compass for Social Change):

- **Organisation Age/Mature Organisations:** Older organisations with more experience and often more capacity can use the macro-level approach to align impact measurement with their grand social change mission. It keeps them focused on their broader, long-term vision.
- **Degree of Social Change/Transformational Change:** Organisations committed to transformational change in beliefs, values, and practices, such as gender equality or human rights organisations, should adopt the macro-level approach. It guides them through complex, long-term journeys. Zahra et al. (2009) call these changemakers "social engineers"; these individuals are aiming for significant social change.
- **Specific Social Mission/Beliefs, Values, and Practices Change:** If your mission revolves around changing societal beliefs, values, and practices, the macro-level approach is essential. It ensures your efforts remain aligned with your overarching mission.

In this structured approach, social entrepreneurs and/or social enterprise managers can consider their organisation age, the degree of social change they aim to achieve, and their specific social mission to determine which lens of social impact measurement – micro, meso, or macro – is the best fit for their unique context and goals.

A Different Approach to Levels of Impact

As well as practitioners (social entrepreneurs and consultants who advise them), researchers are responding to the limitations of the outcomes movement, providing alternative frameworks and models to capture some of the complexities and nuances of measuring impact in the context of complex social change. A recent book by Alnoor Ebrahim (2019) builds on many years of research and practice in this area. Ebrahim recommends fitting the performance measurement system to the type of social mission, taking into consideration level of control over outcomes/impact, and causality between actions and impact. Similar to the three lenses, in this framework impact measurement will depend on the type of social mission. He identifies four different strategies that organisations can follow for performance measurement, depending on the type of social mission. We recommend Ebrahim's book for anyone interested in diving deeper into how to design a performance measurement system that fits different types of social missions.

Box 9.4   Elizabeth Suda, Article 22

So the lesson here is that when you really do take control of your own narrative, and if you can do it in an impactful way whatever that means artistically, elegantly, emotionally, that really is going to be the most long term and strongest benefit. The largest bang for your buck! You can be an advocate for your mission and for your vision, and there's really no one that's better than you to sell that. So, we're all advocates, and I think business is now a space where people can make legitimate change, and they don't need millions of dollars of advertising to do it.

Finally, we hope that these suggestions and frameworks on impact provide food for thought for different audiences. The first audience members are obviously the social entrepreneurs, but beyond them, there are useful takeaways in this chapter for donors, supporters, coaches, educators, and policymakers. We have already mentioned funders, who include grant-givers, donors, and investors, for whom it is particularly important to understand the levels of social change involved in impact, because they have great influence over social enterprises. There is nothing more frustrating for social entrepreneurs than funders who misunderstand the level of change they are working towards. Don't straitjacket your funding recipients into measurement frameworks that are more suited towards service delivery, when in fact they are working to change societal beliefs. It will make a world of difference for funders to work with social enterprises on what would be the most appropriate impact measurement tool or approach for them. Policymakers, umbrella organisations, and other supporters – if you have an appreciation of the range and types of impact that social enterprises are working on, this will help you to understand the ecosystem that you are trying to support, either with services, policy, training, or other offerings.

Conclusion

Social impact can be understood in different ways that we have related to levels of social change. Impact can be a way of demonstrating the effectiveness of your work, it can guide your organisational learning and strategising, and/ or it can be a commitment to a bigger social change that guides all of your work. It is important for social entrepreneurs, supporters, investors, donors, and policymakers to understand these distinctions, in order to take the most effective approach to impact measurement.

References

Ebrahim, A. (2019). *Measuring social change: Performance and accountability in a complex world.* Stanford University Press.
Zahra, S. A., Gedajlovic, E., Neubaum, D. O., & Shulman, J. M. (2009). A typology of social entrepreneurs: Motives, search processes and ethical challenges. *Special Issue Ethics and Entrepreneurship, 24*(5), 519–532. https://doi.org/10.1016/j.jbusvent.2008.04.007

10 Scaling Creatively

Thinking Outside the Toolbox

If you've ever entertained yourself casting ripples in a pond, you know that creating a greater reaction in the water is about much more than just the size of one stone. In the vast pond of social entrepreneurship, the metaphorical ripples of impact extend far beyond mere organisational growth. In Chapter 6, we introduced three different approaches to scaling impact: Scaling up (growing the organisation), scaling out (growing the model), and scaling wide (growing social change) and the challenges associated with each. In summary:

- When engaging in scaling up, there is a potential risk of mission drift as the focus transitions from the original social mission to the expansion of the organisation itself.
- Scaling out poses challenges such as the complexity of measuring progress, constraints in funding, and the requirement for a strategic approach, especially when there is a lack of clear evidence showcasing the impact of the initiative.
- In the context of scaling wide, one encounters a prolonged timeline for accomplishing systemic change, along with the likelihood of minimal financial returns. Additionally, securing support from traditional funders becomes challenging in initiatives directed towards broader social transformation.

Each of these different approaches has benefits and drawbacks, but the important aspect is figuring out when each approach is appropriate, that is, a good fit with the social enterprise and the level of social change implied in its mission. In this chapter we return to those three approaches and explore how social entrepreneurs are finding ways to overcome the challenges, to prioritise social impact, and even to bring about significant social change.

DOI: 10.4324/9781003409694-14

Tying It All Together: When Is Each Approach Suitable?

The key to finding the right scaling strategy is figuring out a good fit between type of social mission and scaling approach.

- Scaling up. Assuming that the social enterprise is ready and able to scale, missions that involve service/product delivery are more suitable to the scaling up approach. If you are successfully delivering a service/product to a local community, you can grow that offering either by offering new services to your existing beneficiaries or by expanding existing services to new beneficiaries. Scaling up strategies for organisational growth are often simpler, with less consideration of power structures and challenging politics and are often better suited to a new social enterprise.
- Scaling out. While all social enterprises benefit from having a Theory of Change, in the case of those that choose to scale out, by sharing their impact model, the disciplined alignment of a Theory of Change will guide new activities that are perhaps side steps, before forward progress can be made to advance the mission. Often after an initial startup phase, social enterprises mature into a social mission that is more complex with a vision that is better served in collaboration with others. This will involve innovative new strategies to disseminate the idea and support other actors.
- Scaling wide. Finally, if the social mission involves significant social change, then a social movement approach is the most suitable. Here, scaling involves the development of existing relationships to increase policy influence, mobilise other actors, and influence societal attitudes. Often, after working on an issue for many years, social entrepreneurs can develop a clearer vision for social change and will undertake activities to enable the whole ecosystem to work towards system change.

Which approach is right for a social enterprise is not fixed and can evolve over time, as the social mission can develop and change. Returning to Zahra et al.'s (2009) typology of social entrepreneurs from Chapter 9 – social bricoleurs, social constructionists, and social engineers – these levels and types of social change can help us understand the three approaches to scaling a social venture. As the authors of that article propose, the three different categories of social entrepreneurs can represent a continuum or a journey. The social entrepreneur starts out by drawing on local knowledge to address an issue (social bricoleur). At this stage, scaling up is a good fit as they can grow their organisation to increase their impact. As they progress their project, they recognise unmet needs and opportunities and are able to respond to them with innovative impact models towards the social change – models that they would like others to share so that they, too, can increase their impact (social constructionist). At that point, they can move into disseminating their success to others and spreading the idea: Scaling out. Ultimately, they may become a social engineer if they manage, after years of hard work, to challenge the status quo with their efforts. If the time is right, and they have mobilised enough people, they may even bring about revolutionary change in the system. Then a scaling wide approach is more suitable to their endeavour.

Here we present methods and tools that social entrepreneurs draw on to bring about transformative change. They come from and relate to a range of different areas of practice and literature and do not fit into one academic discipline. We have gathered approaches that are used by social entrepreneurs around the world. This is nowhere near an exhaustive list, but it gives some insight into how social entrepreneurs are creatively scaling their impact in practice towards social change. These approaches are not well captured in social entrepreneurship literature, which has focused primarily on scaling up (organisational growth) and scaling out (growing the influence of the model collaborating with others who might copy it).

We now focus on scaling wide, which refers to efforts to bring about system change. How do actors in the social entrepreneurship space conceptualise delivering significant social change, which is often referred to and not clearly defined? In Chapter 6, we defined system change as changes in policy, practices, beliefs, legitimacy, and values. We argued that system change does not happen very often, but that social enterprise missions often connect to or are part of a bigger social movement. Scaling social change is a journey on which the social entrepreneur needs the perspective of self-awareness, not only in terms of their own individual strengths and weaknesses but most importantly in terms of where they (and/or their social enterprise) fit in the wider ecosystem of change and resistance to change. Tools that aim towards system change include: Theory of Change, modelling, collaboration, awareness of the ecosystem, and deep democracy.

Calibrating Your Compass: Alignment and Theory of Change

The most important aspect of scaling in all cases and for all social enterprises, as is the case with impact, is alignment. When working towards a social mission, having the guiding star of your vision of a better future is essential for staying on course. Maps are less helpful as the terrain can change, and your course can change along the way. If you want to grow your organisation, grow your influence, and/or work to bring about social change; just make sure that your actions and intentions remain aligned with your mission. As with the other suggestions in this chapter, the compass metaphor recommends process comes before outcomes. In other words, in the journey of social change, how you get there is equally important to where you are going. Having a compass means that you are taking the right path but not necessarily the one set out beforehand on a map.

One practical reason for this emphasis on alignment is that often the legal form of the social enterprise requires the governance and management team to use their resources only on the social mission as stated in the articles of association or constitution of the organisation. The nonprofit social enterprise is legally bound to focus on its mission. The for-profit social enterprise that has BCorp certification must prioritise its mission or lose its BCorp status. The more symbolic reason for alignment is that the defining feature and very identity of a social enterprise is its mission, which guides all of the efforts and towards which resources flow.

Box 10.1   Javier Pita, NaviLens

NaviLens has scaled because it has a good purpose, which is true and which makes companies, institutions and organisations adhere to it because they see that it is real. For example, we do not have investment, nor do we want it because we want to be very faithful to our objective. And our goal is to achieve a better world for people with visual disabilities.

A practical tool that can serve as a compass when scaling is the Theory of Change. As a reminder, the Theory of Change, also called "logic model," is a causal statement that aligns the social enterprise's activities with its outcomes and impact. The structure of a Theory of Change is: If we do X (activity), then we will create Y (output/outcome), which will result in Z (impact). For example, if we train disadvantaged people in employable skills, we will help them to find employment, and we will reduce the amount of unemployment in the area.

In Chapter 5 on impact, we presented the logical model framework. This is the foundation for the Theory of Change and a way to map out its constituent parts. A social enterprise has a Theory of Change to ensure that the planned activities will result in the desired outcomes and wider impact. Scaling with a Theory of Change tests any new activities to make sure that they align with the intended social impact. The social entrepreneur plugs in the activities and required resources to the logical model framework to work through the steps towards outcomes and impact before starting any new initiative. This provides reassurance to supporters and stakeholders that while the activities may be new, they are aligned with the social mission. This can help the social entrepreneur bring stakeholders along with them and potentially prevent resistance.

Modelling a Different Way

One way to demonstrate alignment – to disseminate your mission and "prove" your ideas – is through modelling. Modelling means demonstrating or enacting your values through how you work and what you do. Examples of modelling can be found in the cooperative movement. Cooperatives evolved as an alternative way of organising business relations, where the labourers are usually members who share the profits of the enterprise. A cooperative is an organisational form that may or may not have a specific social mission, beyond the idea of promoting democratic governance structures as an alternative to the dominant shareholder model. While we are primarily concerned here with cooperatives that have a social mission, it is also the case that the cooperative movement in general is, or at least intended to be, an initiative to address power imbalance and injustice in business operations and the global open market. Cooperatives with a social mission, or social cooperatives, in addition to promoting democratic governance, have a social goal. Often, a social entrepreneur will choose a cooperative legal form in order to model equality and fairness, sharing power and profits with collaborators, as did Nguyen Thi Le Na when she set up Phu Quy Agricultural Farm Joint Stock Company.

Another example of modelling is social franchising, an approach that depends on deliberate and formal collaboration. When the social entrepreneur realises that in order to grow impact and include more people in the movement towards change, they will have to go beyond growing their own organisation, they look for ways to influence others, and they encourage others to replicate their idea. The concept of franchising is taken from for-profit business where the franchisor creates a template and set of detailed instructions on how to set up a franchise, so that the franchisee pays to use the business model to make profit but has to strictly follow the rules in order to deliver exactly the same product or service. The reason to set up a franchise is to grow the business, that is, increase profit. In social franchising, which arose in the 1990s, there is a similar contractual arrangement, but the purpose is to spread the social innovation or social service. Social franchising has become particularly popular in rolling out health services especially in economically disadvantaged areas.

Box 10.2   Rodrigo Baggio, Recode

When we started to scale, I looked for models that could inspire me to find the best process to grow and replicate. Finally, we created a model of social franchising to replicate the impact, stimulating people to create their Committee for Democracy in Information Technology (CDI)

> in their territories, while keeping the quality. It then evolved into social networking, which means creating groups of leaders in the regions and exchanging best practices methodology, learning from each other. This is something more special than a regular franchising model. In our case, there is no payment of fees among us, it's collaborative work. Thanks to this social networking model, we can fundraise together for bigger projects considering operations in different countries. So, this collaborative work is good for all the members.

Social franchising is a way of collaborating with others who share your social change mission. The intention isn't to make profit, as with commercial franchising. The drive behind social franchising is to spread the model and coordinate with others how they are all working towards a shared mission. The original social entrepreneur must have established a model that works. They create a template for how to implement that model. Then they have to collaborate with others who are also committed to a shared mission. Social franchising pushes governance to be more deliberative or consultative, and the franchisor becomes more like an orchestrator of knowledge, rather than a simple contractual arrangement of for-profit franchising (Giudici et al., 2020). They may or may not charge a fee to the franchisee. In the case of Rodrigo Baggio above, he does not charge a fee. He passes forward the value that is created through the franchising to others, not aiming to capture it for his own organisation.

Putting It All Together: A Scaling Success Story

Putting some of the tools together, it becomes clear how social entrepreneurship is a journey of organising for social change. Here we provide an example of scaling success: The Cam Vinh Ky Yen orange farm (Truong et al., 2019). In 2013, Nguyen Thi Le Na left her job as Communications Officer in a multinational company and returned to try to save her family's orange farm in central Viet Nam. Russian demand for their product, the Cam Vinh orange, had decreased, and their crop was failing due to soil exhaustion. Le Na set up a new distribution company, Phu Quy Agricultural Farm Joint Stock Company, to find new sales channels and started experimenting with new ways of growing. She discovered that she could get a more reliable, delicious, and sustainable crop if she used organic, syntropic farming, planting combinations of trees and shrubs to combat insects and improve soil quality without the need for chemical pesticides and fertilisers. Once she had established how to farm the Cam Vinh orange sustainably, she trademarked her product and gained certification from the public body: Vietnamese Good Agricultural Practices in 2015. This allowed her to scale up sustainably and find new buyers for her product. Because of her organic syntropic method, she could not rely on a simple linear growth strategy of maximising crop yield; she had to be more creative. So, she scaled out. In 2016, she participated in Oxfam's Enterprising for Development Programme, gaining new skills and growing her network, also collaborating with Japan International Cooperation Agency.

These experiences gave her insight into what it means to be a social impact business and developed a new strategy to scale wide for the benefit of her whole region, not just for the benefit of her own farm and family business. She came up with a plan to partner with other orange farmers, teach them her methods, and become a producer of orange products (jams, sweets, essential oils, tea), which was a new source of revenue but also reduced waste as the bruised or damaged oranges could be used in these products. She obtained investment from Viet Nam Silicon Valley and Thriive Viet Nam to realise this plan by purchasing processing machinery and developing organic farming training programmes for local farmers. In 2018, she went from working with 4 to 29 farmers and had an annual turnover of 1.73 million USD (480 billion VND) in 2019.

While this scaling example looks straightforward, Le Na has faced serious challenges. As a woman, she and her family were criticised and experienced resistance. Her farming methods were rejected by wealthy farmers and farming associations, who did not believe an orange business could work without added chemical fertilisers and pesticides. And she was working in a poor area where the community faced multiple challenges. She continues to grow her social enterprise and is establishing an Eco Village to further support her community, offering training in tourism and hospitality, as well as farming.

The three approaches to scaling are clear in Le Na's journey:

- **Scaling up**: Initially she increased her own crop yield in a sustainable way by applying syntropic organic practices.
- **Scaling out**: She formed new partnerships to develop the business model.
- **Scaling wide**: She disseminated her idea and prioritised growing impact in her community, attaining legitimacy for a different approach to farming in her region to the one that had been considered the "right" way to do it before.

As with all social change, Le Na met with resistance. Deeply held traditional beliefs, practices, and values were a barrier to her mission. She had to navigate her way around these barriers by focusing on the farmers (beneficiaries) with whom she worked modelling a different way, aware of the whole system, with a clear focus on her mission. In order to do this successfully, it is important to be aware of and be able to work with power. The traditional social movement approach is to map the actors in the movement (or ecosystem) and see where the power lies. To learn more about power relations in social missions, we recommend a recent book that redefines power in a practical way as what you have that others want, and how to use that to your advantage (Battilana & Casciaro, 2021).

Box 10.3   João Magalhães, Code For All

The big question when we talk about scaling social innovation is, how can we prepare public entities to adopt our solutions? And it's not about changing the people. Sometimes the decision-makers want to test but they don't have the mechanisms to make it happen. Typically, the problem is about how the processes work. What are the procedures that are already in place that create a huge resistance to adopt any new solution? We need mechanisms where you incentivise testing social innovation. And testing, in the future, may be adopting.

Process over Outcomes: Deep Democracy

There is a growing interest in new, creative, and powerful facilitation methods that focus on the process of how a group is working towards change as more important than the target or goal of change. These methods, such as Presencing (Senge et al., 2008), Theory U (Scharmer, 2016), Systems Thinking (Stroh, 2015), Inner Development Goals, and others, require self-awareness, awareness of the whole ecosystem, adequate time and space, and a serious commitment to the process of change. Deep democracy is one such approach that is taken from psychology and conflict resolution, and has been extensively applied to organisations including social enterprises. It is a concept and approach to decision-making and conflict resolution that seeks to ensure that all voices and perspectives are heard and considered in decision-making processes. It includes a range of different approaches that developed in parallel and have been applied in various fields, including politics, organisational development, and community building. While there are several different approaches to deep democracy, each with its own emphasis and techniques, we focus on two approaches used by community groups and social entrepreneurs in efforts to bring about social change.

Myrna Lewis is known for co-developing the concept of deep democracy along with her late husband, Greg Lewis, based on the teachings of psychotherapist, Arnold Mindell. The Lewis Method of Deep Democracy was based on their work in post-apartheid South Africa, which is now used and applied by practitioners in a wide range of different contexts across the world often with an emphasis on political empowerment. The Lewis approach places a strong emphasis on the exploration of unconscious processes within individuals and groups. It involves techniques such as "experiential conflict resolution" to help individuals and groups uncover and address hidden conflicts and dynamics. The Lewis approach draws from process work, which is a broader psychological framework. It involves working with individuals and groups to bring awareness to their inner experiences, dreams, and emotions, with the goal of integrating these aspects into the decision-making and conflict resolution processes. While this approach is used in therapeutic and counselling settings to help individuals and groups explore and resolve inner conflicts, it is also used by social enterprises and communities to facilitate more inclusive decision-making processes.

Judith Green is known for her work on deep democracy in action in the context of organisations and leadership in the United States, based on her book *Deep Democracy: Community, Diversity, and Transformation* (1999). Green's approach focuses on creating inclusive decision-making processes within organisations. It involves techniques and practices that ensure all voices are heard and considered in the decision-making process. While Myrna Lewis' approach has a broader psychological and therapeutic focus, Judith Green's approach is specifically tailored for application in organisational settings. It seeks to foster more inclusive and participatory organisational cultures and structures. Judith Green has developed specific tools and practices for implementing deep democracy in organisations. This includes methods for effective group facilitation, conflict resolution, and decision-making that encourage open dialogue and diverse perspectives.

These are just two of the many approaches to deep democracy, which can be applied in various contexts depending on the goals and needs of the group or organisation. The common thread among all the approaches is the belief in the value of including all perspectives and addressing hidden conflicts to arrive at more inclusive and effective decision-making processes. In the journey towards social impact, especially when that means significant social change, division and conflict are inevitable. Deep democracy, as with other self-reflective methods, helps to turn that division into a valuable source of meaning, rather than conflict becoming an impasse. Scaling change is possible when people are engaged in the process; but this doesn't happen without very deliberate processes and expert facilitation.

Conclusion

This discussion of scaling – the challenges we saw in Chapter 6 and some tools for advancing scaling in this chapter – show, firstly, how social entrepreneurs are overcoming the challenges of scaling and stretching the concept that originally referred to organisational growth in a profit-making context. Secondly, the range of tools, approaches, efforts, and considerations proves the well-known fact that social entrepreneurs are relentlessly and passionately committed to their social mission and to big ideas of social change.

References

Battilana, J., & Casciaro, T. (2021). *Power, for all: How it really works and why it's everyone's business*. Piatkus.
Giudici, A., Combs, J. G., Cannatelli, B. L., & Smith, B. R. (2020). Successful scaling in social franchising: The case of impact hub. *Entrepreneurship Theory and Practice*, *44*(2), 288–314. https://doi.org/10.1177/1042258718801593
Green, J. M. (1999). *Deep democracy: Community, diversity, and transformation*. Rowman & Littlefield Publishers.
Scharmer, C. O. (2016). *Theory U: Leading from the future as it emerges* (2nd ed.). Berrett-Koehler Publishers.
Senge, P., Scharmer, C. O., Jaworski, J., & Flowers, B. S. (2008). *Presence: Human purpose and the field of the future*. Currency Doubleday.
Stroh, D. P. (2015). *Systems thinking for social change: A practical guide to solving complex problems, avoiding unintended consequences, and achieving lasting results*. Chelsea Green Publishing.
Truong, T. T. N., Cannon, S. M., Picton, C., Sareen, S., & Rhodes, M. L. (2019). *Social enterprises in Viet Nam and Ireland*. Labor Publishing House (Nha xuat ban lao động).
Zahra, S. A., Gedajlovic, E., Neubaum, D. O., & Shulman, J. M. (2009). A typology of social entrepreneurs: Motives, search processes and ethical challenges. *Special Issue Ethics and Entrepreneurship*, *24*(5), 519–532. https://doi.org/10.1016/j.jbusvent.2008.04.007

11 Bringing Ecosystems Together

Think of social entrepreneurship ecosystems like our natural world's diverse and beautifully complex landscapes. Like wild forests, they show their diversity and unique terrain that in the case of social entrepreneurship ecosystems are shaped by the history they carry and local customs. These ecosystems are complex, often incomplete, and as discussed previously in this book, face some important challenges:

- Managing diversity: One significant issue is the clash between striving for the neatness of a normative approach and embracing diversity.
- Overlapping ecosystems: The social entrepreneurship landscape intertwines with other ecosystems, including traditional entrepreneurship and the social economy.
- The role of government: The power dynamics between the public and private sectors will condition some critical qualities of the social entrepreneurship ecosystem.
- Governance challenges arise, causing confusion and fragmentation: Not all places have well-established private organisations to represent social entrepreneurship or engaged public administrations.
- Imbalance of resources: Prosperous cities benefit more from these ecosystems than rural regions. Even within the same city, certain groups may be left struggling for support.

We will now discuss some ideas that try to work with the complexity of social entrepreneurship ecosystems which, like the diverse ecosystems in the natural world, are better served if driven by the celebration of diversity and embracing life's intricacies.

DOI: 10.4324/9781003409694-15

Navigating the Social Entrepreneurship Ecosystem

Box 11.1   Javier Pita, NaviLens

Society and institutions help you, and in the end, you feel very supported, which has been a fundamental part of our success. For example, the foundations that have awarded us prizes, the society that has supported us, the associations that have helped us, the users that have helped us, the companies that have helped us. It is wonderful to see how everyone wants to be part of creating something better for people with disabilities.

If you are a practitioner, it is very important for you to be aware of the ecosystem around you and all the players involved, even the ones that might not be obvious to you immediately. As we discussed in Chapter 1, social entrepreneurship has emerged from different traditions in different communities in different regions. Most people are likely to see players who share their same tradition as relevant and be somewhat oblivious to the rest. This would be a huge mistake. It is safe to assume that they are all there for a reason that stems from the historical evolution of the issue you are trying to solve and of the way in which solving that issue evolved in your context. Social entrepreneurs should kick things off by recognising and celebrating the wide range of perspectives and worldviews in these ecosystems. Does that mean we need to take everything at face value and can never evolve our ecosystems? No, but, as all systems thinkers will tell you, beware of changing a system that you don't fully understand. From that positive attitude towards the diversity of actors, you will be ready to dive in.

As ecologists study species' interconnectedness in an ecosystem, social entrepreneurs should recognise tribes and overlapping systems in theirs. Many players that are relevant for you won't even be a part of the social entrepreneurship ecosystem, but they might be an important part of yours, given the issues you are trying to solve. Mapping all the actors around the issue you work on will give you a more complete and complex picture. Be comfortable with this complexity because it is real although not so neat. Seeing the reality of the space in which you work will be more helpful than simply staying around those who share your own take on social enterprising.

To make things more complicated, you can't simply categorise actors in the ecosystem by legal form. The multiple legal forms that social enterprises use often won't help you understand the type of animal they are in ways that matter to you. For example, you might not be so interested in knowing if they are incorporated as a foundation or a limited company as in knowing what methodology they use to reforest or to foster labour inclusion.

Once you have identified categories of actors defined in ways that are valuable to you, consider that not all actors within the same category materialise in the same way across contexts. In other words, it is not enough to put tags on organisations: This is a labour inclusion firm, an impact investor, an agricultural cooperative, and so on. It serves social enterprises well to be much more nuanced than that. Just as various organisms in the natural world adapt to their environments, behaviour within social entrepreneurship ecosystems is highly context dependent. In this case, the context, as mentioned before, might not be geological but historical, social, political, or economic.

This attribute of natural living things that also applies to organisations was beautifully explained by Economy Nobel Prize Laureate Elinor Ostrom (2010):

> "Individual differences do make a difference, but the context of interactions also affects behavior over time (Walker and E.Ostrom 2009). Biologists recognize that an organism's appearance and behavior are affected by the environment in which it develops. "For example, some plants produce large, thin leaves (which enhance photosynthetic photon harvest) in low light and narrow, thicker leaves (which conserve water) in high light; certain insects develop wings only if they live in crowded conditions (and hence are likely to run out of adequate food in their current location). Such environmentally contingent development is so commonplace that it can be regarded as a universal property of living things. (David W. Pfenning and Cris Ledón-Rettig 209:268).""

In nature, the same species will develop various adaptations to a given context to succeed in it. In the same way, in a social enterprise ecosystem, the same kind of actor, say an impact investment fund, might take a somewhat different form in a given environment than in another one. If we take a closer look at impact investment funds, some tend to be "impact-first," and they are more patient when it comes to financial returns. Others might look more like a traditional venture capital fund albeit with a social and/or environmental impact purpose. Similar to how there will be more likelihood of finding one version of a natural species in one environment than another, impact investors will also be more likely found in one shape or another in various places depending on context.

Just as the amount of light available in a forest conditions the kind of leaves a given species of a plant grows, so will the nature of impact investors depend on the kind of money they are able to attract. If an impact fund is attracting money that was originally earmarked for philanthropy, for the investors in the fund it will make sense to be impact-first. They will be happy with a longer-term return, as they used to get none. If an impact fund is attracting money that was originally earmarked for financial investments, the investors in the fund will expect returns that are comparable to what they used to attain, and this will put shorter-term pressure on the financial performance for the fund managers.

Of course, the kind of money fund managers attract depends on the investment thesis they make to investors. But in coming up with the investment thesis, fund managers run into contextual conditions that shape their chances of being successful at fundraising. The reality is that not every country has a strong philanthropic tradition, and not all private investment scenarios develop in the same way. It depends on the country, its history, and its economy. Ultimately, the kind of money that is available in each context for these impact funds is not something the fund can always choose. Just like plants don't choose the nutrients available wherever it is that their seeds are dropped by a bird, the same logic can apply to many other types of players.

Box 11.2   Chris Gordon, ISEN

We like to think that network support organisations for social enterprises and social economy communities are all the same, with a traditional membership structure. But our findings from the Net-Works project funded by Erasmus+ funding told us a different story. From funding to supports, from activities and events to the purpose of setting them up in the first place, they all vary.

Once you have an idea of the actors' true nature and can understand and appreciate them for what they are, you also need to see the ways in which they engage with each other. As discussed in Chapter 7, the ecosystem you are in normally lacks a single governing body. There may or may not be a relevant role played by the government; if there is, the government level involved in the specific issue you care for might be national, regional, local, or a combination of several. Private actors may or may not be organised in associations (one or several), and their roles will vary from country to country. This means there will always be some organic, informal relationship system around you that you need to learn about and work with.

To work with the ecosystem, once you get your head around it (or think that you do), you must ultimately ask yourself, what is my role and/or that of the social enterprise I'm involved with in this particular ecosystem? Please note how this is very different from asking yourself what your competitive advantage is as compared to others in the ecosystem. Your final goal is to solve a social/environmental problem, and you probably share this same goal with many of the organisations you have mapped as relevant in your ecosystem. How can you leverage and add to the ecosystem in ways that are conducive to solving the problems you have set to solve?

Box 11.3   Elizabeth Suda, Article 22

We are very strong collaborators with the artisans that we work with as well as the nonprofit sector, with Mines Advisory Group and others . . . And we donate to them to create this ecosystem where there's expertise. Article 22 is not an expert in land clearance, but we do know how to communicate the story through jewellery. That sort of collaboration is a very respectful way of operating; it is operating with the sense of "power with" not "power over." It's really about looking at each collaborator's expertise and putting that together to celebrate everyone's work and advance towards the same goal.

Fostering a Collaborative Ecosystem

In this section, we aim to share our views on how to go about catalysing collective efforts to solve social/environmental problems by contributing to the ecosystem. By its very nature, social entrepreneurship is at the crossroads of various institutional logics. In this lies its beauty and in this lies the complexity of structuring a somewhat stitched ecosystem around it. If you are part of an organisation of the social entrepreneurship ecosystem (impact investor, accelerator, crowdfunding platform, etc.) and made it through the book to this point, you might already know what we are about to discuss. Don't you?

Let us not deceive you and first mention exactly what you expect us to say. It is paramount that all actors in the ecosystem embrace diversity and hybridity in all its shades as intrinsic values. When it comes to entrepreneurial ecosystems, think of them as complex systems. In simpler terms, this means that everything happening in the big picture is influenced by how all the system players interact. As stated by Klimas and Wronka-Pośpiech (2022), "One property of complex systems is that as the diversity of a system's components increases, the system becomes more resilient." Consider that, just like in nature, more diverse ecosystems are more resilient. Isn't that why we need to protect biodiversity? It is interesting how we see certain things clearly in nature and then forget about them when looking at ourselves (and, arguably, also the opposite). Preserving diversity and fostering collaboration across different sectors and institutions is the key to building a resilient ecosystem. This collaboration can only be effective when rooted in sincere appreciation and respect for the role of others who are different from us.

Here we add a caveat, because life is complex. In the world of organising for social change, there are often serious, difficult, and traumatic reasons to fight for change. Frequently, it is those who have been historically oppressed, denied their human right to exist as full equal humans, who organise (and fight) for social change. Therefore, in your ecosystem, there may be actors who have fundamental ideological differences. In such a case, mutual appreciation and collaboration are not straightforward, maybe even not possible at all. Such social change falls under the area of transitional justice, where a variety of tools have been shown to be effective: Formal processes acknowledging human rights abuses, reparations, reconciliation dialogues, truth commissions, to name a few. We cannot cover these in detail here, but it is important to note that ecosystems around social entrepreneurship can overlap into this challenging space as well. The basic advice is the same – know your context, know your social issue, and be aware of all the actors involved.

Some may think of a natural ecosystem as a static, sealed greenhouse. That's far from being the case. Natural ecosystems have blurry, porous boundaries. They are constantly changing, dynamically influenced by external and internal factors and actors. Just as the boundaries between ecosystems in nature are porous and overlapping, social entrepreneurship ecosystems should encourage interaction between different actors. It is that porousness that enables new, more resilient, and fitting species to evolve in nature. The same logic applies to social entrepreneurship.

We already mentioned how the social entrepreneurship ecosystem often overlaps with the social economy and traditional entrepreneurship ecosystems, illustrated in Figure 11.1. This might not happen to the same degree in all countries, depending on the historical evolution of their social economy movements and how developed their venturing ecosystem is, but it will to some extent. And this is great for all. Social entrepreneurship can learn from both, and surely other actors in these ecosystems can find value in engaging with social enterprises. Due to their nature, some social enterprises will fall 100% under the social economy. Others will be very aligned with the traditional entrepreneurship space. And many will be in between both spaces.

This might be a good time to pause and reflect on your own thinking. Maybe what we just described made sense to you. Or maybe not. Did you just think that the previous is a ridiculous statement because, obviously, all social enterprises are part of the social economy and not traditional entrepreneurship? Or, on the opposite, did you just think that the previous is a ridiculous statement because, obviously, all social enterprises are part of the traditional

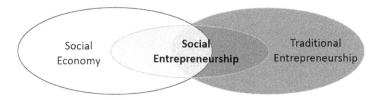

Figure 11.1 Overlapping ecosystems

entrepreneurship ecosystem, and the social economy ecosystem pertains only to traditional nonprofits? These thoughts are the glasses through which you see the world, conditioned by the tradition and reality of the region/country/community where you have grown professionally and personally. Maybe you haven't had the chance to see the social economy as a vibrant, innovative movement, but others have experienced it as such. Maybe in your country, the entrepreneurship ecosystem is very developed and nourishes diverse options, including impact-first, but in others, it isn't. Be aware that "obviously" is a term that seldom applies to social entrepreneurship. Figure 11.1 allows you to zoom out and see how three ecosystems intersect. Social entrepreneurship can sit within the social economy ecosystem, within traditional entrepreneurship ecosystem, or somewhere in the middle.

Once you truly appreciate the ecosystem to which you have set yourself to contribute, consider your role within it. Going back to Gonzalez and Dentchev's (2021) categories: Are you the fuel that drives change, the hardware that provides support, or the DNA that carries the ecosystem's genetic code? Of course, there will be actors doing several of these things, but you get the point. Recognise the importance of each role, as different stages of social entrepreneurship may require different contributions. The first two will usually be more important earlier on in the social entrepreneurship process, and the third one is always important. Just as in nature, diverse roles and functions contribute to the ecosystem's resilience.

Box 11.4   João Magalhães, Code For All

Having this ecosystem helps a lot when you're starting. Then when you scale up sometimes, I feel that the ecosystem doesn't see you anymore as the typical social enterprise. And so when you grow, it changes a little bit, and it's more about finding your space in the middle of these nonprofit and for-profit spaces.

As in the case of social enterprises, also for other actors in the ecosystem, it is not a question of competitive advantage versus other players but a question of additionality of value, leveraging from the discussions in previous chapters about impact. For those providing fuel (financial institutions, research organisations, volunteers, etc.) and those providing hardware (practical tools, working spaces, legal advice, etc.), are you really adding value, or are you offering more support to the social enterprises that already have backing? Addressing ecosystem inequities such as the rural–urban divide or resource constraints where social entrepreneurship is needed most is critical. For example, supporting youth ecosystems might require somewhat different approaches such as working with influencers who encourage creative problem-solving and evolving the evaluation standards for funding youth-led initiatives to better align them with the broader benefits of youth social entrepreneurship (Bublitz et al., 2021).

Box 11.5   Chris Gordon, ISEN

When you want to support social enterprises, you must provide a range of options. This problem comes up with networks. Are you helping pre-startup organisations, startup or established organisations? Are you concerned with scaling and international organisations? Then, are you helping social care or education social enterprises, are you helping digital entities, just transition focused entities? All of these entities need differing supports. And so, with a network you need to think on providing services that everyone is affected by, or you do a deep dive on a particular sector or topic.

If you are driving the ecosystem's cultural and policy aspects that impact social enterprises, what kind of direction are you setting? Is it one that celebrates and recognises diversity? Policies, laws, and financial tools should be designed to support hybrid models. To use a concrete example, in some countries there might be the temptation to create the one legal form under which all social enterprises must fit. Then, if you are not incorporated in this way, your government and ecosystem won't recognise you as a social enterprise. This would be a big mistake. It would reduce diversity and hybridity and damage the ability of social enterprises to adapt to what might be required to solve different challenges in different places (Neverauskiene & Pranskeviciute, 2021). The best legal frameworks are those that offer a diverse enough array of legal structures that social enterprises can choose from such that each can use the one that works best for their missions.

Ultimately, if we want to make a real difference, we need to focus on developing the whole system and encouraging new players and ways of doing things. We need to "stimulate the emergence of missing actors or behaviours, support the creation of cross-sectoral collaboration and self-support networks" (Neverauskiene & Pranskeviciute, 2021, p. 43). Without losing sight of the fact that a complete ecosystem is going to look different in different contexts.

A Short Note on Ecosystem Governance: Polycentric Governance for Thriving Social Entrepreneurship Ecosystems

As discussed, diverse actors collaborate and specialise in a healthy ecosystem, increasing support availability. The quality of this support hinges on ecosystem governance and structure, which should enhance the interactions among actors to foster synergies and boost assistance for social enterprises (Diaz & Dentchev, 2021). We already discussed in Chapter 7 how falling into the temptation of expecting the government to come and save the day can, provided you happen to successfully convince the government to do so, damage the ecosystem's diversity, resilience, and local relevance. So, it's vital to strike a balance.

Government support should facilitate, not dictate, the growth of social enterprises. Striking this balance empowers social entrepreneurs and ensures that they retain their legitimacy in the eyes of the public. In more self-organised ecosystems, where initiatives are diverse and localised, governments should consider a supporting role, recognising the inherent strength of grassroots efforts. In contexts in which self-organisation is lacking, government should be more proactive and support the development of the ecosystem.

In a balanced ecosystem (which would necessarily materialise differently in different contexts), governance is a complex and dynamic challenge. Inspired by the work of Elinor Ostrom, we would like to spark your interest in the concept of polycentric governance as an effective approach to managing the intricate interactions within these ecosystems. Polycentric governance, a term coined by Ostrom, implies the existence of many centres of decision-making that are formally independent of each other. The essential characteristic of this approach is that these centres function interdependently, forming a web of relationships crucial for the efficient functioning of a complex system.

Conditions for successful polycentric governance within social entrepreneurship ecosystems include actors knowing one another, effective communication, the development of shared agreements and norms, and the ability to aggregate predictions. When these conditions are met, a polycentric governance model can facilitate a thriving ecosystem where diverse actors, including government entities, nonprofits, universities, and social enterprises, work with each other to achieve common goals. This approach acknowledges the interdependence of these actors and leverages their diverse perspectives and resources to foster the growth of social entrepreneurship ecosystems and the positive impact they generate. As such, polycentric governance is a valuable framework that can guide policymakers and ecosystem builders in creating dynamic, resilient, and collaborative social entrepreneurship ecosystems.

Conclusion

In the untidy world of social entrepreneurship ecosystems, acknowledging history, celebrating diversity, and understanding the dynamic interactions between actors are core building blocks. Just like nature's varied species adapt to their environments, social enterprises and other players in the ecosystem take different forms influenced by their context. And that adaptability, which brings about diversity, is critical for the resilience of the ecosystem.

We should all be asking ourselves, what role should I play in catalysing collective efforts to tackle societal challenges? So, embrace complexity, address inequalities, and nurture the entire system to make a real impact.

References

Bublitz, M. G., Chaplin, L. N., Peracchio, L. A., Cermin, A. D., Dida, M., Escalas, J. E., & Miller, E. G. (2021). Rise up: Understanding youth social entrepreneurs and their ecosystems. *Journal of Public Policy & Marketing, 40*(2), 206–225.

Gonzalez, A. D., & Dentchev, N. A. (2021). Ecosystems in support of social entrepreneurs: A literature review. *Social Enterprise Journal, 17*(3), 329–360.

Klimas, P., & Wronka-Pośpiech, M. (2022). Social entrepreneurship and entrepreneurial ecosystems: Do they fit? *Problemy Zarządzania, 20*(1(95)), 43–66.

Neverauskiene, L. O., & Pranskeviciute, I. (2021). Hybridity of social enterprise models and ecosystems. *Journal of International Studies, 14*(1).

Ostrom, E. (2010). Beyond markets and states: Polycentric governance of complex economic systems. *American Economic Review, 100*(3), 641–672.

Pfennig, D. W., & Ledón-Rettig, C. (2009). *The flexible organism.*

Walker, J., & Ostrom, E. (2009). Trust and reciprocity as foundations for cooperation. *Whom can we trust, 91124.*

Conclusion
The Real Promise, as We See It

We hope to have inspired in you, dear reader, our appreciation for the power of social entrepreneurship in shaping a more just and sustainable future. In this book, after outlining the captivating promise of social entrepreneurship, we confronted the challenging realities that social entrepreneurs face and then explored ways forward. We truly believe that the promise of social entrepreneurship is enriched by looking at it with realism and depth. As we stand at the crossroads of conclusion, let's roll up our sleeves, transform intentions into deeds, and shape the future we envision.

We wish for this book to serve as a call to action, inviting each reader to take these insights and apply them to their own endeavours, whether as social entrepreneurs, researchers, policymakers, or individuals interested in organising for positive change. We will now explore how different people might use the learning of this book.

Box 12.1   Javier Pita, NaviLens

Do you remember the movie "Slumdog Millionaire?" [SPOILER ALERT!] It tells the life of a boy who answers the questions of a TV programme using the learnings of different moments of his life. Sometimes positive, sometimes difficult. I always say that NaviLens is the fruit of all those challenges and difficulties that we have had. All that learning is what has made my life what it is today.

Caring for the Social and Environmental Value Creators

If you've read the book up to here, you've already got the main messages. In a nutshell, as a social entrepreneur, you must take care of yourself and your team. If you are an actor in the social entrepreneurship ecosystem, you need to make sure to help social entrepreneurs do so. But the experiences of social

DOI: 10.4324/9781003409694-16

entrepreneurs offer insights that can benefit individuals well beyond the social entrepreneurship community.

In larger corporations, the shift towards incorporating goals beyond profit maximisation, such as becoming purpose driven or contributing to environmental and societal well-being, has far-reaching implications for the people involved. This transformation of business strategy stems from a heightened awareness of the complexities that shape our world. In this new landscape, the experience at work of corporate employees and leaders shares some traits with that of individuals in the realm of social entrepreneurship. Are you in such a transformative corporate setting? If so, the lessons offered in this book are relevant. Recognising the human aspect in balancing financial, social, and environmental goals and fostering individual and team welfare are key drivers of lasting change, whether within a social enterprise or a purpose-driven corporation.

If you are in the third sector, you will have realised already how these learnings can be very directly applied. Nonprofits working across different causes can benefit from nurturing strong team dynamics, recognising the value of diversity within their teams, and making sure to manage talent professionally. By adopting these principles, we can navigate challenges more effectively and work towards greater well-being as we promote a sustainable future.

Impact: Knowing What Difference You Are Making in the World

We have reviewed what the literature says about social impact (Chapter 3), the importance of considering the different types of missions (Chapter 5), and finally, how to find a good fit between the approach to social/environmental impact and the type of mission and social enterprise you have (Chapter 9). The important message in that journey is self-awareness. Impact can mean accountability, it can mean organisational learning and strategic development, and it can mean social change. What does it mean to you? No matter what area you work in. Is your purpose to develop your career within the status quo? Then you would be interested in high-quality work and good practice. Is your purpose personal and career development? Then you might take a more learning-oriented strategic development approach. If you have a purpose that is a commitment to some kind of social change, whether that is protecting the environment or fighting for social justice, then you have a social change mission and you need to be aware of the challenges and opportunities that can bring.

There is a growing interest in self-awareness and self-reflection practices, encouraging us to see the connection between our personal situations and global trends and practices. Many have written about this increased level of consciousness in organisations (Macy & Brown, 2014; Senge et al., 2005; Wheatley, 2006). It is as though we are growing up as a species and realising that we are responsible for ourselves and our world. You could argue that this reflects an over-inflated sense of agency; what can one person do to combat such huge and wicked problems as growing socio-economic inequality or climate crisis? Maybe it's naiveté? And there are plenty of people who will take this cynical view. But you could also take it as noble that more people are waking up to their own role in shaping the systems in which they are a part.

Scaling: How to Grow Impact

The key takeaways on scaling social enterprises are that you should always ask yourself: What are you trying to scale? We have scaling up methods where the assumption is that you are scaling organisational size in order to scale impact. The scaling-out approach talks about scaling social impact by disseminating an innovative model that other organisations might implement. And finally, a scaling wide approach focuses on how to bring about systemic changes in societal legitimacy by increasing your influence and network. So, once again, scaling is not a straightforward concept. The assumption is often that you should scale without reflecting on what, why, or how. We have argued that you have to know what you want to scale, and then figure out the process of how to scale it, and there are some methods that can engage wider groups of people to be part of scaling positive impact, such as deep democracy.

The issue of how to bring your community along with you or engage authentically and respectfully with a diverse group of stakeholders is relevant to a wider audience. Anyone working in a democratic or inclusive organisation who sees an appetite for more self-aware organising can bring in training on more participatory practices, such as the ones we have recommended. There are many methods and consultants to support your work. Importantly, start with articulating the social mission if it isn't already clear; that can take a long time but it is worth getting this foundational step right. Agreeing on a focus can be a source of conflict, but with the right process method, that conflict can be an important source of learning, rather than a source of division.

Bringing Ecosystems Together

Throughout the book we have stressed the importance of acknowledging history, celebrating diversity, embracing complexity, and understanding the dynamic interactions within ecosystems in every possible way we could imagine. Social entrepreneurs can directly apply these learnings to navigate their ecosystems effectively, leveraging them to better advance their missions. Understanding and embracing the different players in the field can lead to more resilient and innovative solutions to social and environmental problems.

But we are convinced that this wisdom is highly relevant to a variety of actors in society. For policymakers and government officials, understanding the dynamic interactions within ecosystems can assist in developing more effective policies for social and environmental challenges. Cross-sectoral collaborative networks can directly apply the principles of polycentric governance to enhance collaboration and support across different sectors. By recognising the interdependence of diverse actors, they can create more resilient and effective ecosystems for addressing complex societal and environmental problems.

The Role of Academia and Future Research

Since both the authors work in leading European business schools, we can't finish this book without discussing the specific role of higher education institutions and specifically business schools in social entrepreneurship. Of course, all education institutions play critical roles in fostering social entrepreneurship. We believe that some, like primary and secondary education, play an even more important role than ours. However, you will understand that we can't refrain from picking apart our own space. Thank you for bearing with us while we do so. We promise it won't take long.

Universities hold a pivotal position in nurturing the growth and sustainability of social entrepreneurs, their organisations, and ecosystems. Their role transcends the classroom and extends into the real world of social entrepreneurship. Education is the foundation for nurturing future social entrepreneurs and strengthening their organisations and ecosystems. Universities can become innovation hubs that empower aspiring social entrepreneurs with essential tools to succeed (Kim et al., 2020). As business schools, are we approaching entrepreneurship education and our own entrepreneurship ecosystems with a modern, diverse, and purpose-driven mindset? Is it easy for social entrepreneurship to flourish and find specialised support within our ecosystems? Or are we stuck in the 2010s and the idea that nothing that doesn't look like Facebook will make us proud? Not even Facebook wants to be Facebook any longer. Come on, don't be so 2010!

Research in social entrepreneurship can also contribute immense value. However, in case you are not in academia, let us break the news to you: Social entrepreneurship is not an easy space for researchers. In academic research, we are fond of strict definitions, and we tend to operate in silos. This is often driven by the need to publish in specific journals and the (limited) capacity of some journals to accept cross-disciplinary approaches and exploratory fields. Kudos to so many researchers who navigate this complex space without surrendering their commitment to social entrepreneurship!

This space needs as much scientific knowledge as it can get. Producing research that can really be helpful for social entrepreneurs also involves harnessing insights about their pitfalls. Are there specific mishaps that they need to be particularly prepared for? Or, thinking of social entrepreneurship ecosystems, we need to know more about the factors that facilitate their development, the role of government policy in fostering them, and inequalities across and within, just to name a few topics.

Finally, encouraging cross-sectoral collaboration is something that comes naturally to universities as (relatively) neutral actors where all others can feel welcome. Business schools, like all other higher education institutions, should be a melting pot where hybridity is natural and various traditions find a place. By encouraging different sectors to work together and fostering networks of mutual support, academia contributes to a more resilient and collaborative ecosystem.

A Conversation Starter: The Real Promise, as We See It

In our quest to navigate the promise, pitfalls, and the way forward in social entrepreneurship, we realise that we have posed many questions that remain unanswered and uncovered ongoing debates to which there is no easy closing. The journey is far from over, and the dialogue around social entrepreneurship's promise, pitfalls, and potential will continue to evolve. As we conclude this book, let us finish by opening a new conversation rather than closing it.

Social entrepreneurship has huge promise and potential, although it may differ from what researchers, funders, practitioners, and policymakers envisioned two decades ago. Which, by the way, was completely different for different researchers, funders, practitioners, and policymakers. Since the early days when different approaches to social entrepreneurship emerged separately around the world, there has been a diverse plurality of voices, experiences, perspectives, and initiatives, across the political spectrum and from different disciplines. While there may have been fragmentation initially, the trend that we have seen since then has been a blurring of boundaries between the different approaches in practice.

This is why we say that social entrepreneurship's time has come. In the early days, it was perhaps equal parts naïve and brave to think that a change-maker could actually bring about a significant social change. Now the field has matured to have a theoretical basis (to some extent), a history (or histories), and an evidence base (many empirical studies by researchers and consultants). In this book, we have tried to fairly and accurately present many of these different perspectives and draw from numerous traditions, not just one. We have participated deliberately in this blurring of boundaries between different approaches. Appreciating the value that different perspectives bring is how we recommended interacting with ecosystems in Chapter 11, so we are following our own advice here. We see it as promising that the various approaches are coming together, making the field's future look bright indeed. So, social entrepreneurs (and policymakers, funders, and supporters) no longer need to be only naïve and brave but also can be informed and armed with various models, theories, and tools derived from different traditions. They can be prepared and can find a support network.

Our current wider cultural context is characterised by division, information wars, misinformation, and polarisation. Driving this tangled mess is the phenomenon called the "culture wars": Taking sides based on ideological positions or group identity. Nowhere is this clearer than in debates about the climate crisis. In the midst of the culture wars, where entrenched ideological divisions often lead to rigid positions and intractable conflicts, social entrepreneurship emerges as an alternative to picking sides in warring camps. While social media debates tend to drive people to their respective corners, social entrepreneurs and social enterprise managers can find value in various perspectives and draw insights from them, ready as they are to roll up their sleeves and use all the tools at their disposal to make a tangible difference.

Those involved in social enterprises are deeply committed to their work, very connected to specific social and environmental issues, and driven by a desire for real-world impact. These attributes enable them to break through the inertia of ideological polarisation by focusing on evidence-based solutions, not just rhetoric, and collaborating in an ecosystem of diverse stakeholders. Their strong commitment to specific social or environmental missions offers the possibility of moving beyond the divisions that have paralysed progress in the past to focus on solutions. This is the real promise of social entrepreneurship as we see it.

References

Kim, M. G., Lee, J. H., Roh, T., & Son, H. (2020). Social entrepreneurship education as an innovation hub for building an entrepreneurial ecosystem: The case of the KAIST social entrepreneurship MBA program. *Sustainability*, *12*(22), 9736.
Macy, J., & Brown, M. (2014). *Coming back to life*. New Society Publishers.
Senge, P., Scharmer, C. O., Jaworski, J., & Flowers, B. S. (2005). *Presence: An exploration of profound change in people, organizations, and society*. Currency Doubleday.
Wheatley, M. J. (2006). *Leadership and the new science*. Berrett-Koehler Publishers Inc.

Index

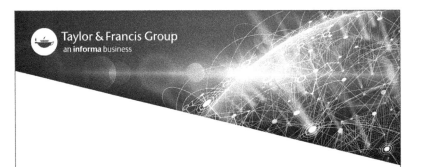

For Product Safety Concerns and Information please contact our EU
representative GPSR@taylorandfrancis.com
Taylor & Francis Verlag GmbH, Kaufingerstraße 24, 80331 München, Germany

www.ingramcontent.com/pod-product-compliance
Ingram Content Group UK Ltd.
Pitfield, Milton Keynes, MK11 3LW, UK
UKHW021823240425
457818UK00006B/53